OXFORD
INDIA SHORT
INTRODUCTIONS
**PUBLIC POLICY
IN INDIA**

The Oxford India Short
Introductions are concise,
stimulating, and accessible guides
to different aspects of India.
Combining authoritative analysis,
new ideas, and diverse perspectives,
they discuss subjects which are
topical yet enduring, as also
emerging areas of study and debate.

OTHER TITLES IN THE SERIES

Dalit Assertion
Sudha Pai

Political Economy of Reforms in India
Rahul Mukherji

Coalition Politics in India
Bidyut Chakrabarty

Mughal Painting
S.P. Verma

Pathways to Economic Development
Amitava K. Dutta

International Trade and India
Parthapratim Pal

Indian Foreign Policy
Sumit Ganguly

The Indian Middle Class
Surinder S. Jodhka and Aseem Prakash

Labour in Contemporary India
Praveen Jha

Bollywood
M.K. Raghavendra

Citizenship in India
Anupama Roy

For more information, visit our website:
https://india.oup.com/content/series/o/
oxford-india-short-introductions/

OXFORD
INDIA SHORT
INTRODUCTIONS

PUBLIC POLICY
IN INDIA

RAJESH CHAKRABARTI
KAUSHIKI SANYAL

OXFORD
UNIVERSITY PRESS

OXFORD
UNIVERSITY PRESS

Oxford University Press is a department of the University of Oxford.
It furthers the University's objective of excellence in research, scholarship,
and education by publishing worldwide. Oxford is a registered trademark of
Oxford University Press in the UK and in certain other countries

Published in India by
Oxford University Press
22 Workspace, 2nd Floor, 1/22 Asaf Ali Road, New Delhi 110 002, India

© Oxford University Press 2017

The moral rights of the authors have been asserted

First Edition published in 2017

19th impression 2025

ISBN-13: 978-0-19-947069-3
ISBN-10: 0-19-947069-3

Typeset in 11/15.6 Bembo Std
by Excellent Laser Typesetters, Pitampura, Delhi 110034
Printed in India by Manipal Technologies Limited

Contents

Preface   IX
Prologue   XI

1   Public Policy in India: Past and Present   1
2   Policy Formulation: Processes and Players   35
3   Policy Implementation: Framework and
    Challenges   72
4   Policy Analysis and Evaluation   109
5   Strengthening Policymaking in India   139

Epilogue   168
Bibliography   171
Index   177
About the Authors   195

Preface

For a subject that is central to most of media coverage in the country—outstripping even cricket and Bollywood—public policy in India suffers from a drought of books. This gap is felt even more acutely because given its special nuances of colonial history, administrative challenges, and a highly distinctive political culture, international books scarcely cover the policy realities of the country. So when Oxford University Press (OUP) approached us to write on the subject for the Oxford India Short Introduction series, we jumped at the opportunity.

Our attempt in this short introduction has been to strike a balance between rigour and accuracy on the one hand and accessibility on the other. We have applied a simple structure of formulation, implementation, and evaluation to span the subject. We have tried to present a fair amount of recent research.

For a multidisciplinary field like public policy, any choice of boundary would be necessarily arbitrary and there is absolutely no claim of comprehensiveness here. We have tried to serve up an appetizer rather than a sumptuous meal, to part the curtains to allow a glimpse rather than provide an all-encompassing survey of the landscape.

We owe a huge debt to the team at OUP, as well as the referees, for shepherding the volume through on a strict timeline. We alone are responsible for the errors that have doubtless escaped the scrutiny of many pairs of eyes.

Public policy is too important a matter to be left to policymakers alone. Our aspiration here is no less than bringing about greater appreciation of and participation in public policy in India, to contribute to the process of replacing heat with light in the area. To the extent that the volume kindles interest in the reader to further explore the fascinating subject, we shall consider our efforts amply rewarded.

Prologue

It was a chilly November morning in Patna. The year, 2005. Nitish Kumar, the newly elected chief minister (CM), had called Abhayanand, a senior Indian Police Service (IPS) officer with impeccable reputation for integrity, intelligence, and innovative thinking, to his temporary residence for an early morning meeting. Kumar's top challenge in fixing Bihar was law and order. The state was on the brink of lawlessness, where politically connected hoodlums roamed in jeeps brandishing firearms in open daylight. Kidnapping was fast becoming the state's signature industry. People in the capital feared to step out after dark. There was no hope of turning Bihar around without fixing law and order. Kumar hoped Abhayanand would know how to do it. (See Chakrabarti 2012.)

'Police *ka rutba dikhaiyen*' (establish the authority of the cops), the CM asked. In turn, Abhayanand could get whatever he needed—funds for more personnel and better weapons or equipment, or tougher laws to put suspects behind bars. Abhayanand declined both, asking only for political non-interference instead. He knew what Bihar needed.

In the three years that followed, Bihar's law and order took a sharp turn for the better, enabling a virtual rebuilding of the state on all fronts: from laying new roads to running better schools and health centres, making Bihar one of the fastest growing states of the country. All this was accomplished within the confines of law—without 'encounters' (or custodial homicide staged as exchange of fire), without custodial excesses, without any extra-legal action. It was a policy coup!

How did Abhayanand pull it off? His strategy involved cold rational assessment of the situation, identifying two key innovative solutions, and implementing these solutions with the tenacity of a bulldog. His diagnosis was unconventional: he knew that the broken link in law and order was neither police investigation nor arresting criminals, but keeping them behind bars. With abysmal conviction rates, arrests had just lost their teeth as a deterrent. His prescription: flawless and timely post-arrest paperwork—'speedy trials'. Conviction rates soared. Within months, word began to get around that something had changed in Bihar.

Second innovation was equally counter-intuitive. He focused on prosecuting one offence—what then seemed almost a traffic infraction—possession of illegal firearms. The timing was tricky: he did this at a time when *bahubalis* with charges of murder, rape, kidnapping, and dacoity ruled the streets. Nevertheless, it was also among the most easily prosecutable of offences and could get people locked up for three to five years. Furthermore, it was almost a prerequisite for other, more heinous crimes. In two short years, Bihar had locked up more people on this single charge than on all the others combined. (See Chakrabarti 2012 for a discussion.)

However, just finding the right solution was only half the story. Implementation did not happen just because Abhayanand ordered it—even in as hierarchical a system as the police force. Abhayanand pushed his superintendents and monitored them continuously, personally calling them up every evening through late night, checking status, providing advice on the law, supporting and often virtually retraining them to go the entire length to translate his innovations into action. Also, constantly adjusting and course-correcting as the strategy met ground reality. Without this unrelenting focus on implementation and adjustment, even the most brilliant of policy innovations would have had negligible effect on the ground.

Public policy is a matter of life and death—of people, societies, even the entire world. It determines the quality of ordinary citizens' lives, the prosperity of nations, peace, security, and sustainability at a geo-political level. It makes the difference between breakout nations and failed states. At its heart lie scientific principles of logical analysis of reliable data leading to accurate formulation. Equally critical is the most complex and challenging task of implementing it, negotiating a vexing maze of organizational psychology and human systems in a fast-changing environment. Some say it is much like fixing an airplane in flight.

1

Public Policy in India

Past and Present

Public policy is a relatively young discipline, although its practice, one may argue, is as old as civilization itself. In this chapter, we trace concisely the emergence and boundaries of the field of public policy as a discipline and its evolution in India. We then look at some of today's defining policy issues to get a sense of the coverage of the field.

The Field of Public Policy

The birth of management and public policy as accepted domains of research and training has been among the major twentieth-century developments in the social sciences. They have much in common—both are essentially multidisciplinary and have a strong component and burden of 'practical relevance'. Both are also primarily American creations.

Emergence of fields of knowledge, like most evolutionary processes, is difficult to date precisely. Nor is there complete consensus about their founders. Just like management, public policy as a regular field of study trailed practice by centuries, if not millennia. Among the earliest recorded voices advocating for the need of a separate branch of study of public administration from the traditional concerns of political science was none other than that of the future US president, Woodrow Wilson. He had famously observed in the 1880s: 'It is getting harder to run a Constitution than to frame one.' The time for the idea had clearly come: a wave of public administration departments started in several major US universities in the late nineteenth century, with their curricula looking surprisingly similar to what would soon be taught in business schools after Harvard launched the genre in 1908: budgeting and accounting methods, finance, standardization of procedures, performance assessments, and industrial organization. The goal was achieving efficiency in administration, rather than worrying about the political objectives and machinations.

The quest for bringing 'scientific methods' into matters of public concern continued, leading to the landmark publication of *The Policy Sciences* (1951) by Harold Lasswell (considered by some as the father of public policy) and Daniel Lerner. By then, the field had broadened significantly to include the policymaking process. The first schools of public policy as opposed to public administration had just begun to emerge in several leading US universities. The distinction was more than nominal—while public administration was understood to be delivering policy goals set by political authorities unquestioningly and with utmost efficiency, the field of public policy was wider. It questioned the very justifiability of the policy goals themselves, analysing their suitability to broader national and human values. Formulation and analysis of policy now joined, and soon began to overshadow, the unadulter-ated quest of efficiency in implementation.

Explained literally, 'policy' refers to a rule—a guide to decision-making. Hence, any rule that affects the public at large, or people, or all members of a com-munity, is the subject matter of public policy. In the paragraphs that follow, its key territories are outlined.

Few among the many definitions of public policy available in literature can beat this one in brevity and sweep: 'Whatever governments choose to do or not to do' (Dye 1992). (See Cairney [2011] or Stone [2012] for a list of definitions.) It is undeniable that at its core, public policy has always been about governance. What are governments really supposed to do? The almost definitional duty of government is to ensure law and order, and defence. It is hardly surprising then that some of the oldest treatises on public policy—from Sun Tzu's *The Art of War* to Chanakya's *Arthashastra* to Machiavelli's *Prince*—have all tended to focus on the provision of public administration or battlefield strategies. Naturally, law and jurisprudence have been key topics of interest in public policy.

Another equally fundamental practice in public policy is of international trade and its inevitable corollaries—regulation and trade disputes. Moreover, taxes are essential for governments to survive. Thus enters economics, providing the analytical tools of direct economic decisions of the government. It also provides a cost–benefit framework that helps choose

4

between alternatives using a clearly stated policy objective.

Defence and trade considerations have also necessitated diplomacy since ancient times, making international relations a critical area of study in public policy. Other social issues that often dominate public debate today—like health and education, whether in the form of 'ObamaCare' healthcare plan in the US or the Right to Education in India—made their appearance with the emergence of the 'welfare state' in the nineteenth century. It was for the first time that these services began to be increasingly seen as state responsibility.

More recently, environmental issues have emerged as key elements of government decision-making around the world and they have also quickly found their place in the public policy discourse. A grasp over rapidly changing technology and its disruptive impact is imperative for both policy planning and execution.

For emerging market economies, the subject of economic development—from infrastructure creation to poverty reduction—which is generally seen as a key public good and responsibility of the government, comprises yet another key area of policymaking.

In terms of processes, policymaking involves three major steps in an unending cycle: (a) formulation or crafting of policy to best serve its stated goals; (b) implementation or the day-to-day putting to action of the policy; and (c) evaluation or analysis to understand how well it has worked and why, leading to future improvements in formulation and implementation.

Policy implementation requires the mastery of an entirely different skillset, essentially that of efficient management. The ability to motivate a large number of people; to direct, supervise, organize, and course-correct them dynamically to ensure timely completion of desired projects is important. For instance, deciding on and funding the laying of the Metro railway in Delhi was a major policy decision that involved complex analysis, but its execution on time and within budget was arguably an even bigger challenge. (The overlap of skills for public policy and management has been long recognized, at least in the West. It is interesting to note that the iconic Harvard Business School was originally proposed to be a school for management and public administration.)

But even that is not enough. Policymakers also need to master a highly intricate political process, inherent in building consensus, carrying a large number of people along, and compensating groups that bear the brunt of the 'greater good' (for instance, the villagers who lose their homes and fields for a major dam project initiated for supplying irrigation and electricity to a region). In the old 'policy sciences' paradigm, the Holy Grail for public policy was efficiently maximizing national welfare defined in an almost purely rational manner—a job for well-trained and brilliant technocrats. The concomitant political hurly-burly was considered unavoidable background noise that policy experts should largely ignore.

However, over time, it became clear that in a democratic setting, the policymaker can ignore a famously fickle electorate only at his own peril, since neither are the goalposts constant nor is his tenure guaranteed. Politics, therefore, is more than just a sanctioning environment; it is also the vital connect between the shifting needs and desires of the populace and the policymaker. Public policy therefore needs to be broader than a pure rational search and managerial execution of an optimum strategy for a clearly defined problem. It must include a dynamic exercise of being constantly in harmony with the ultimate client—

the populace. Communication skills—listening and articulating—as well as in-depth understanding of ground politics are highly critical.

Which disciplines and academic areas does the field of public policy cover today? At a risk of over-generalization, a glimpse at the curriculum of three major graduate programmes in the world—The John F. Kennedy School of Government at Harvard University, Massachusetts, US; Sciences Po, Paris, France; and the Lee Kuan Yew School of Public Policy, National University of Singapore, Singapore—may shed some light on this question.

University departments and policy schools, how-ever, are not the only places where policy research and advocacy occurs. Decades before the emergence of the first public policy school, in 1916, a businessman named Robert S. Brookings established an epony-mous think tank that started a genre of institutions which time and again played a key role in critical areas of policymaking. The Brookings Institution itself, for instance, is associated with the setting up of the Congressional Budget Office and several other notable initiatives. Others like the Carnegie Endowment, the RAND Corporation, and the Liberty Institute—either

TABLE 1.1 Subjects and Specializations in Three Major Public Policy Programmes

University	Subjects	Specializations
Harvard (North America)	• Economics • Ethics • Management and leadership • Negotiations • Politics • Policy analysis • Quantitative analysis	• Business and government policy • Democracy, politics, and institutions • International and global affairs • International trade and finance • Political and economic development • Social and urban policy
Sciences Po (Europe)	• Public economics • Public policy • Ethics • Technology • Management • International governance • Law	• Public administration • Cultural policy and management • Digital, new technology, and public policy • Economics and public policy • Energy, resources, and sustainability • Global health • Management of public affairs • Social policy and social innovation
Lee Kuan Yew (Asia)	• Policy challenges • Policy process and institutions • Policy analysis • Economic foundations for public policy	• Economic and policy analysis • Politics and international relations • Social, environmental, and urban policy • Public management and leadership

Source: Respective university websites.

non-partisan or with explicit ideological leanings—have functioned in the twilight zone of the academia and government, conducting research and using it to influence policy.

Public Policy as a Field in India

The development of public policy as a field in India is still in its early stages. (For an excellent exposition of this idea, see Chaudhuri [2016].) This somewhat belies the initial promise of the intellectual–policymaker entente of the Nehruvian era. Nehru was famously open, and indeed seeking, of scholarly policy inputs from intellectuals from various disciplines—P.C. Mahalanobis, Homi Bhabha, and V.K.R.V. Rao being great examples. However, after the Nehruvian era, the connection between academic experts and actual policymakers grew progressively weaker. The Planning Commission that Mahalanobis helped set up eventually became the brains trust of policymaking in India, but, by its very nature, the commission was singularly focused on economic matters. Moreover, inspired by the Soviet Union, it created a highly centralized policy edifice.

Post Nehru, policy ideation was gradually monopo-
lized by the bureaucracy. For several decades, the
politico-bureaucratic combine had an interesting
sharing of roles where the political class—often not
formally educated enough to handle nuances of
complex policy debates—focused solely on winning
power. The business of administration and ideating
for policymaking was largely left to the bureaucracy,
which, in turn, grew increasingly insular to external
inputs. The only group of scholars who continued
to have some influence were economists—from I.G.
Patel and Sukhomoy Chakravarti to Arjun Sengupta
and Raja Chelliah. Social scientists from all other fields
were largely ignored. This was as much because of the
centrality of economics to policymaking as it was to
the somewhat technical nature of the subject putting it
beyond the reach of the non-economist IAS officers.

The increasing insularity of the bureaucrats to
policy experts notwithstanding, attempts at promoting
institutions of public policy were not altogether absent.
The strong connection between management and public policy observed in the US also held true for India
as the very first two Indian Institutes of Management
(IIMs), established in the early 1960s at Calcutta

(now Kolkata) and Ahmedabad, quickly developed a strong interest in public management. IIM Calcutta had the public policy and management group, and IIM Ahmedabad (IIMA) introduced the public systems group. Nevertheless, neither of these groups managed to progress beyond creating a multidisciplinary group of faculty for offering these programmes. It was the third IIM in Bangalore (now Bengaluru) which established a Centre for Public Policy (CPP) as late as in 2000. The CPP started the first postgraduate programme on public policy and management (PGPPPM) in 2002.

The CPP was the result of a tripartite agreement between the Department of Personnel and Training (DoPT), Government of India; the United Nations Development Programme (UNDP); and IIM Bangalore (IIMB). Over the past couple of decades, there has been a reinvigorated attempt by the central government to provide mid-career training to bureaucrats and give them opportunities to study public policy in a long degree-equivalent programme. The DoPT sponsors public policy education of many of its interested officers in major institutions abroad, including at Harvard's Kennedy School of Government. Other than IIMB, similar programmes have also been introduced at the

Management Development Institute (MDI) and The Energy and Resources Institute (TERI) University.

In 2007, IIMA joined the field with its one-year postgraduate programme in public management and policy (PGP-PMP) but the programme had to be discontinued after three batches owing to a limited demand from the bureaucrats. The existing DoPT-supported programmes have also largely failed to excite the bureaucrats, owing to their full-time nature. Till recently, private sector interest in and funding of public policy research and education has been virtually non-existent in India. The reason is not hard to find. Privately funded research institutions of any kind are a rarity in the country (Tata Institute of Fundamental Research [TIFR], Tata Institute of Social Sciences [TISS], and Indian Institute of Science [IISC] had private origins [initially funded by the Tata group] but are now government funded). As for teaching, career opportunities in public policy have been severely limited owing to the practice of the government to hire permanent staff only through the Union Public Service Commission (UPSC) and state Public Service Commission (PSC) examinations, which have little to do with public policy training.

13

The situation began to change somewhat with liberalization. Ironically, as the stifling grip of the government on the economy loosened, the need for public policy education and research began to be felt. It is hardly a secret that the key to business success in independent India traditionally lay in managing the government well. During the days of the permit/licence raj, government officials had power of life and death over private business. For many sectors such as infrastructure and natural-resource dependent industries like mining, things have not changed drastically even in the quarter century of liberalization.

Management of relationships with government remains critically important today, even though the nature of the industry–government relationship may have changed over time. Meanwhile, deregulation and opening up to foreign direct investment (FDI) have increased the number of domestic players as well as major global businesses in several sectors. Consequently, a need has arisen in the private sector in India for people who are not only trained in traditional management but also have an understanding of the practices and priorities of government officials, in order to develop mutually beneficial relationships with the corporates.

Over the years, India has witnessed the arrival of global non-profits like Oxfam and ActionAid along with a growth of non-governmental organizations (NGOs) which now require people with specialization in public policy for their advocacy needs. It is, perhaps, as a reaction to this changed scenario that public policy programmes have witnessed a significant interest from privately funded institutions in recent years. The O.P. Jindal Global University at Sonipat, Haryana, offers a master's programme in public policy. The Bharti Institute of Public Policy also introduced a part-time mid-career management programme in public policy (MPPP) at Indian School of Business (ISB) in 2015. In the same year, IIMA announced the launch of its JSW School of Public Policy with plans to re-launch its programme in public policy.

Apart from public policy education, the sector has also seen the emergence of several think tanks such as Brookings India by Brookings Institution, and Carnegie India by Carnegie Endowment for International Peace, its sixth international centre. The Hindu Group has launched its own public policy think tank—the Hindu Centre for Politics and Public Policy. Many other think tanks which were established earlier like the National Council of Applied Economic Research (NCAER), Indian Council for Research on International Economic Relations (ICRIER), Centre for Policy Research (CPR), India Development Foundation (IDF), the Institute of Defence Studies and Analyses (IDSA), Centre for Civil Society (CCS), and the Observer Research Foundation (ORF) all look at various issues of public policy. According to the University of Pennsylvania's 2016 *Global Go-To Think Tank Index Report*, India ranked fourth globally with 280 think tanks, after the US (1835), China (435), and the UK (288).

The recent emergence of non-government players in the public policy space signify a welcome new trend for India—the reduction in the degree of government monopoly over public policy thought. While the government is, almost by definition, the formulator and implementer of public policy, in an effective democracy the thought and debate informing policy formulation should necessarily extend beyond the confines of government bureaucracy. This can happen when either the bureaucracy reaches out to external experts for their inputs or when experts give analysis in media by using facts and figures, influencing public opinion. That is how public policymaking becomes more informed and gets progressively based on evidence.

An unquestioning government monopoly over policy thought is the surest recipe to policy disaster. This is particularly true for the third step of the policy cycle—analysis and evaluation of policy outcomes. Independent evaluation of policy is a key element of healthy policymaking, and the operative word here is 'independent'. This is an area where India has been especially weak. The notion of independent evaluation of government policies is a relatively new idea in India, introduced only in the first decade of the new century and there is still a significant lack of clarity and serious paucity of capability to carry out thorough evaluations. The bureaucracy in India has always been notoriously insecure about getting policy outcomes independently evaluated (Chaudhuri 2016; Weiner 1979a, 1979b), understandably so since the findings may affect the careers of individual bureaucrats.

The entire idea of conducting research to assess policy needs or evaluate policy measures is typically blocked on the grounds that the needs or results are self-evident, or with the blanket charge that the researchers are 'too academic'. Even when such a study is commissioned, given that the funding for most research institutions is government controlled, its independence is seriously compromised. The government invariably manages to find ways to suppress unfavourable findings. External research inputs rarely find any application in policymaking.

The only solution is to develop a culture of evaluations for private players to fund policy analysis and research so as to develop capability to actually evaluate policies and projects, and to require government projects to be mandatorily evaluated by neutrally funded agencies, and to make the reports publicly available.

A Bird's-eye View of Major Public Policy Debates in India

With the evolution of the field of public policy as a discipline as well as its rise in India already traced, this section aims to take a closer look at the actual content and focus of the field as it applies to contemporary India. Given the strong connect of policymaking with several sectors and disciplines, it is helpful to categorize the hundreds of ongoing policy debates around a few broad and enduring principles. However, this is not a simple task as none of the various frameworks can provide comprehensive coverage or watertight segmentation. Nevertheless, one can use Harold Lasswell's basic definition of public policy as 'who gets what, when and how' as the starting point for this exercise.

We need to realize that every single policy decision produces winners and losers, and therefore, has supporters and detractors. It is for the decision-maker to balance the interests of various competing groups over scarce resources; and between the principle of individual rights and collective welfare. In doing so, there needs to be clarity over the policy objective, the 'north star' of the policymaker. Mahatma Gandhi's famous talisman about recalling the face of the poorest person is one such objective. Another goal is provided in the Preamble of the Constitution, which resolved 'to secure to all its citizens: JUSTICE, social, economic and political; LIBERTY of thought, expression, belief, faith and worship; EQUALITY of status and of opportunity; and to promote among them all FRATERNITY assuring the dignity of the individual and the unity and integrity of the Nation'.

With these broad policy goals in mind (and noting the absence of economic prosperity among them), a few selected policy debates are flagged in this section to get a sense of the nature of public policy issues. Choosing simplicity over comprehensiveness, only two principles are used to characterize a few debates—resource/rights allocation between competing groups and balancing individual right with collective/national interest.

Clearly, not every policy decision entails one or both of these two choices. Many policies—for instance, a foreign policy question about whether or not to align with a global power—are driven by pure pragmatism and the choice of the easiest route to a pre-defined policy goal.

Distributive Justice

In 2011, news broke out that Andhra Pradesh and Tamil Nadu had issued more below poverty line (BPL) cards than the then population of those states. This clearly indicated that many of the cards were bogus, that is, issued to non-existent people. The BPL card is used to avail benefits from different government schemes in the states, such as subsidised food grains, fuel from the Public Distribution System (PDS), low cost treatment in hospitals, and access to housing.

A few years ago, in a run-up to the Right to Food Security, a muted but serious debate raged among the policy intelligentsia about the massive fiscal burden that the law would impose on the State. Accusations of impropriety and corruption in the allocation of coal blocks and 2G spectrum, invalidated by the Supreme Court, contributed in a big way to the exit of the United Progressive Alliance (UPA) in the 2014 general election. In 2015, the newly elected government in Delhi under the Aam Aadmi Party (AAP), kept its poll promise, and slashed power tariffs by 50 per cent and gave free water up to 20,000 litres a month to residents of Delhi. The cost to the exchequer was estimated to be Rs 16.7 billion. In early 2016, after an extremely destructive Jat agitation shook Haryana, the government agreed to add the caste for special reservations within other backward classes (OBC). Within a fortnight the high court of Punjab and Haryana stayed the execution of the order. (See Anand [2007]; Chakrabarti and Sanyal [n.d.].)

While these debates, controversies, and decisions may look unique at first glance, they are actually

21

indicators of a broader resource allocation problem. There are no easy or universal answers to these issues. Take, for instance, the food security issue: the problem can be looked through the lens of efficiency or equity or even a mix of the two. Should the government subsidize foodgrains for the majority of the population? Is that an efficient use of limited resources? Does that deprive other competing needs such as education, health, and security from resource allocation? Is the right population segment being subsidized? Would there be any externalities of the scheme such as adverse impact on the environment and water table? Do the public administrators have the capacity to implement the scheme? Can we easily identify and punish the violators? How are we serving the principles of justice and equality in the Preamble of the Constitution through the decisions? The other examples also have their own bouquet of such questions.

For a slightly nuanced variant of the problem of resource allocation, consider the decade-long fight over the bauxite-rich Niyamgiri Hills in Odisha. Vedanta Resources, through its subsidiary, Sterlite India, had a joint venture agreement with Odisha Mining Corporation to mine the Niyamgiri Hills for bauxite. But the Dongria Kondh tribe, which resides in the area, refused to let them mine the hills since it held them sacred. What is more, they actually emerged victorious with the help of some activists and international NGOs. They even appealed to James Cameron, the director of the film *Avatar*, for lending his voice on their behalf since his film dealt with the subject of protecting tribal land from mining.

On the one hand, the dilemma raises questions about customary rights of tribals against individual property rights. On the other, it raises questions about who benefits from these developmental activities and who pays the price. Are the displaced tribes adequately compensated and rehabilitated? Are the benefits of economic development also going to the tribal population directly affected by displacement? What rights do they have over government-owned land? Should mining be completely stopped in certain areas? If so, how would that impact India economically? How much resources should be allocated for the welfare of the tribal population and how should these resources be deployed?

These issues are not merely economic in nature. The Niyamgiri dispute also highlights the sociological issue of the uneasy relationship between tribal cultures and the mainstream idea of modernity. Do we preserve the socio–cultural ethos of the tribal population at the cost of denying the majority population the benefits of bauxite mining? Do we educate the tribal children in mainstream schools to integrate them better into the larger society and give them a chance towards economic prosperity? Alternatively, do we focus on preserving the tribal way of life, which possesses many positive aspects such as concern for the environment and gender equality but lags in other aspects? All these are difficult questions.

What does justice mean in the context of resource allocation? How should the decision-maker choose between equality (sameness) and equity (fairness)? In 2007, Tehelka reported an interesting study conducted by researchers of the Indian Institute of Dalit Studies. The study found that 'if you applied for an entry-level job in the corporate sector with a name like Ramdas Chamar or Mohan Paswan, and also sent a résumé as Badrinath Shrivastav or Sundaram Iyengar with the same set of credentials, the applications bearing the distinctly Dalit names (Chamar/Paswan) are less likely to get a response' (Anand 2007). Caste-based discrimination persists even today, consciously or otherwise. How much of support does a traditionally disadvantaged person deserve? Are reservations the best solution? At what point does it incite communal clashes like the Jat outrage? In reference to the Preamble, where should the line between justice and fraternity be drawn?

Balancing the Individual's Rights with National/Collective Interest

India became the first country to ban Salman Rushdie's controversial novel, *The Satanic Verses,* in 1988. In 2003, it banned a book on the Maratha ruler Shivaji, *Shivaji: Hindu King in Islamic India* by James Laine, an American professor, on the ground that it hurt Maratha pride. In 2012, two young girls were arrested for posting content on social media, criticizing the shutdown of Mumbai city after the demise of Shiv Sena leader, Bal Thackeray. However, the two girls were eventually released and the Supreme Court struck down section 66A of the Information Technology Act, under which they were arrested. In February 2016, the president of JNU's students' union, Kanhaiya Kumar, was arrested on the charge of sedition. In the JNU case, most legal luminaries weighed in on the side of free speech stating that mere sloganeering does not amount to sedition. However, the Delhi High Court, while granting six months bail to Kumar in March, made him give an undertaking that he would not 'actively or passively' participate in such an activity again and in its order held that the slogans could not be protected as fundamental right to freedom of speech and expression. (See Mathur 2016.)

India's constitution guarantees freedom of speech and expression to its citizens even as it imposes certain 'reasonable restrictions'. Thus, speech that threatens security of the state, public order, decency and morality, maintenance of friendly relations with foreign states, as well as those that amount to contempt of court, defamation, and incitement to an offence can be disallowed. However, as the incidents above illustrate, the fundamental right to free speech has remained an intensely contested space. Rarely has the political class upheld the principles of free speech in the face of mob violence, and it has never hesitated to slap charges on activists who have spoken out against government policies. The 'reasonable restrictions' on free speech have been described as 'vague and overbroad' but little consensus exists on the matter (Tang et al. 2015).

Intertwined with the issue of free speech is that of secularism. With the memory of the horror of partition, India's founders chose to establish a liberal and secular democracy where protection of minority rights was given a pride of place. As per the 2011 census, Muslims are the largest minority religious community (13 per cent), followed by Christians (2.3 per cent), Sikhs (1.9 per cent), Buddhists (0.8 per cent), and Jains (0.6 per cent). The Constitution guarantees the right to practice and propagate any religion of a citizen's choice subject to public order, morality, health, social welfare, and reform. It also allows religious and linguistic minorities to establish and administer educational institutions, and institutions for religious and charitable purposes. While India does not have a state religion, it added the word 'secular' in its Preamble with the Forty-second Constitutional Amendment in 1976. Secularism, as defined by courts and practiced in India, does not mean a rigid separation of the church and the state as practiced in the US and some countries in Europe. It simply means that the state is equidistant from all religions.

However, religion has played a divisive role in many ways. While Nehru had emphatically brought about many progressive reforms in the Hindu personal laws relating to marriage, inheritance, and adoption, similar reforms were not considered politically feasible in the personal laws of several the other religions. Over three and a half decades later, the Rajiv Gandhi government actually overturned a Supreme Court judgment (*Mohd. Ahmed Khan* v. *Shah Bano Begum and Ors* 1985 SCR (3) 844), which had awarded Shah Bano, a 62-year-old Muslim woman with five children, the right to alimony from her husband who had divorced her. This, in turn, became the rallying cry of the Bhartiya Janata Party (BJP) against minority appeasement. To appear balanced, the administration of the day allowed Hindus to pray in the long-locked-up Ram Janmabhoomi–Babri Masjid structure at Ayodhya, lighting the fuse of a long, violent, and destructive political cycle leading to the destruction of the Masjid and causing riots that costed scores of lives around the country. Such are the implications of wrong policy decisions.

The issue of rights of religious minorities is a challenge in most multicultural countries: no one has the perfect track record in the matter. Free speech poses hard questions for other countries as well. According to a 2015 survey of 38 countries conducted by Pew Research Center, Washington, DC (Wike and Simmons 2015), majority of citizens in these countries supported criticizing government policies but they were less supportive of any speech that called for violent protest, was offensive to a particular religion, or was sexually explicit. The US stood out as the most supportive of free speech, followed by Canada, France, Germany, Spain, and the UK.

The survey illustrates why governments across the world cannot always take a consistent and hard-line position on free speech and censorship. Leaving aside political expediencies, citizens themselves are divided on this issue, which makes it necessary for governments to take matters on a case-by-case basis. Some of the questions that need to be weighed before a decision is made include the following: Who or what is being criticized? Whom is it offending? Is the speech merely provocative or can it incite violence against a group? Does curtailing of the 'offensive' material serve the larger public interest? Does it add to the knowledge base of a country?

Lasswell's Last Question: 'How?'

How do these policy questions get settled? Who gets to decide on these issues? Who authorizes them? The next chapter takes an in-depth look at these questions. It is pertinent to remind ourselves that in a democracy like India, the ultimate authority of policymaking lies with the elected legislatures (union parliament and state legislatures) that elect, authorize, and monitor the executive (the council of ministers) from among themselves. The executive governs the country with the bureaucracy.

Elected representatives have to ensure their re-election, which makes it difficult for them to take unpopular decisions and tempts them into populism. There also exists the practice of so-called 'pork-barrel' politics, which unfairly favours the minister's constituency. Besides, certain policies require deeper technical knowledge than what legislators may possess. Finally, as popular civil society agitations have demonstrated, the sense of citizens of being adequately represented by the legislators is also fast eroding.

Some parts of decision making—conducting monetary policy, overseeing various technical parts of the financial system, or telecoms—are carried out through independent regulators, distant from the politics of the day. Finally, rules that govern politicians themselves— elections, and division of fiscal powers between centre and states—are carried out through constitutionally mandated commissions like election commission and finance commissions. Even the governments consult committees of experts on technical and contentious issues.

The authority of the elected legislature, however, cannot run contrary to the constitution, the funda- mental rule book of the country. The judiciary is the final interpreter of the Constitution. Over the years, the judiciary has often held government orders and even laws unconstitutional and, in response to Public Interest Litigations (PILs), even driven the bureaucracy to perform its duty when it believed it has failed its constitutional role. Much of the rights-based laws that passed in the two terms of the UPA government origi- nated from judicial orders; be it the National Food Security Act (NFSA) or the Right to Education Act, the judiciary played a crucial role. The fact that work- places now have to mandatorily constitute committees to investigate sexual harassment cases came from the famous *Vishaka* judgment (*Vishaka and Ors* v. *State of Rajasthan and Ors*, 1997 (6) SCC 241. In this judgment, the Supreme Court laid down specific guidelines on the prevention of sexual harassment of women at the workplace. The legislature later enacted a law on the matter).

However, these acts by the judiciary could also be seen as encroachment on the role of the administrative and legislative function of the executive. Aside from the issue of blurring of separation of powers, judicial activism, while well intentioned, can sometimes be counter-productive with implementation challenges since, generally speaking, not a wide range of stake-holders get their voices heard in court. For example, in 1998, in its effort to reduce pollution in the capital, the Delhi High Court imposed a cap on autorickshaw licences. This led to a black market of issuance of licences, coupled with significant commuter hardship owing to shortage of autorickshaws on the road.

Significantly, the massive failure of the state to deliver public goods efficiently and equitably has become a subject of study all its own. Scholars and activists alike have suggested various reforms—ranging from computerization and e-governance, to making specific public officials accountable for their omissions and commissions. The Karnataka government's 'Sakala' initiative, which guarantees public services to citizens within stipulated time, is an example of reforms through e-governance. Another example is the Right to Information (RTI) Act, which fines specific officers for delaying delivery of information beyond the stipulated period.

Elected representatives have the difficult task of ensuring delivery of services through the vast bureaucracy over which it has little control, except the power to transfer them. The bureaucracy, on the other hand, has to endure political interference in its duties. Some issues that need to be analysed well are the following. Is there a case for re-thinking the structure of the bureaucracy and its accountability mechanisms? What methods could be employed to incentivize both elected representatives and the bureaucracy to perform their duties in a fair and efficient manner? What methods could be employed to minimize corruption, especially at the lower bureaucracy level?

The present near-adversarial relationship between the judiciary and legislature need introspection. To what extent is judicial activism acceptable? What are the pitfalls of judicial activism? Conversely, what methods could be employed to make the executive more responsive to the needs of the citizen? How accountable is the judiciary to the other organs of the state? Since it is an unelected body, how competent is the judiciary to pronounce on matters in the legislative domain?

While this chapter may have highlighted a few key public policy issues and their underlying trade-offs, this is by no means a comprehensive list of issues. Public policy is an endless process as changing times keep throwing up new choices and challenges.

How do policies actually get made? Who are the key players in the process? What is the timeline of policy change? How do the checks and balances of a modern democracy operate in India and with how much success? These are the questions that are explored in the next chapter.

2

Policy Formulation
Processes and Players

India's Constitution has explicitly banned forced labour and child labour in factories and for other hazardous work. However, both these malpractices were rampant even during the 1980s and the 1990s and have only declined (not disappeared) because of sustained campaigning and focused legislation. More than half a century since Independence, khap panchayats still mete out clearly illegal and inhuman 'judgments' against young couples in broad daylight, with the support of a significant majority in villages. Media surveys routinely reveal rabidly patriarchal and feudal mindset of the law enforcers of the nation.

Clearly, mere edicts from policymakers cannot bring about the desired societal change. Any policy needs to be formulated in a way such that it sticks around, by persuasion, incentive, and, if necessary, by taking punitive measures against lawbreakers. Policymakers also have to be skilled negotiators to be able to bargain with a cross-section of actors—political parties, legislators, bureaucracy, NGOs, and other interest groups. Formulating the correct policies and developing consensus around them is critical.

It is also maddeningly complex and, more often than not, contentious. Solutions to policy problems are rarely free of side effects. Policymakers have to balance interests of a wide range of stakeholders, think of the most efficient way to allocate scarce resources, and ensure that the policy itself is implementable at the ground level. How do they do this task? Who are the players and institutions involved in the process? What role do they play? Is the process context-specific and iterative? What makes a policy successful? This chapter aims at addressing these questions.

Theorizing about the policy formulation process started in the 1950s, almost exclusively in the West. However, no single definitive theory can explain all aspects of policymaking process in a nutshell. Each new theory builds on and complements other existing theories. The research questions determine what aspect of the policy process a specific theory focuses on. The 'stages' model developed by Harold Lasswell and B.D. Jones was one of the first theories that described policymaking as a linear and rational process. Charles Lindblom's 'incrementalism' view of policymaking came next. It applied the concept of bounded rationality, and held the view that policymakers 'muddle through' by making only small changes from existing policies.

The depiction of the policy process driver began to change from a distant rationalist to a political entity with Paul Sabatier's 'advocacy coalition framework' (ACF) in 1988. The ACF contends that groups with shared beliefs (technical expertise and ideology) form 'advocacy coalitions' that coordinate advocacy activity following the emergence of a particular policy question on the government agenda. These coalitions consist of legislators, interest groups, public agencies, policy researchers, journalists, and other sub-national actors. The ACF helps explain change in the policy process by arguing that advocacy coalitions engage in 'policy-oriented learning'. These groups continually adapt to changes in the political and socio-economic environment and revise their preferences in policy designs and goals based on the new information.

Other recent theories include the 'punctuated equilibrium framework', which characterizes periods of intense policy action as well as the lulls, by changes to the tone of an issue, and 'multiple streams approach', which holds that a policy action happens at the confluence of three streams: problems, policies, and politics. To what extent these theories apply to the Indian context is a matter of empirical research.

Broadly, there are five stages in the policymaking process, of which three constitute the formulation part. However, the process itself is not linear. As policies are implemented, shortcomings in their formulation or implementation or new problems are identified and added to the policy agenda. Figure 2.1 describes the various stages of policymaking. Policies are shaped within the framework of a country's constitutional system. In India's case, three features stand out most prominently: the parliamentary form of government; federalism and a broad band of social, economic, and political philosophy articulated in the preamble; and the directive principles of state policy and fundamental rights. (See Figure 2.1 for a brief explanation of these terms.)

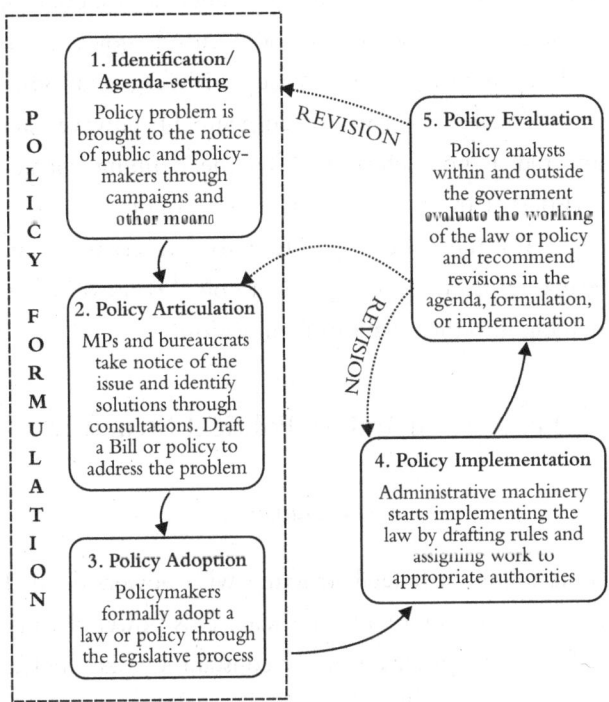

FIGURE 2.1 Process of Policymaking
Source: Adapted from 'The Texas Politics Project', https://texaspolitics.utexas.edu/archive/html/bur/features/0303_01/policy.html, last accessed on 27 August 2016.

Policy formulation necessarily involves various persons and institutions operating in hierarchical or consultative roles, including groups in government like ministers, civil servants, parliamentarians, political parties, judiciary, as well as those outside government such as media, pressure groups, NGOs, and other professionals. The rules of engagement, however, are affected, if not determined, by the defining characteristics of the national policy and political environment. It is therefore helpful to go over a few pertinent structural features of the Indian policy context before delving into the details of formulation.

Features of India's Political Structure

Federalism

India follows a federal structure with powers divided between the centre and the state. This power sharing is, however, neither equal nor constant. Unlike the US where the states chose to give up certain powers to the federal government, in India, the central government shared certain powers with the states but kept the lion's share with itself. This stems from the need for a strong centre to help a diverse people evolve into the concept of nationhood.

Law-making power is also divided between the two levels. Subjects are divided into three lists—union, state, and concurrent. For example, defence, railways, and income tax are in the union list; trade and commerce, fisheries, police, and health are in the state list; and electricity, education, drugs, and newspapers are in the concurrent list (both centre and state can legislate on these subjects).

Separation of Powers

The legislature, executive, and the judiciary are the three organs of the state (see Table 2.1 for a snapshot of the structure). The legislature is the law-making body, the executive is responsible for the enforcement of such laws, and the judiciary deals with interpretation of constitution and cases of breach of law. The three branches are expected to exercise their respective powers without overstepping their limits. The basic idea behind the doctrine of separation of powers is to have a system of checks and balances to prevent the abuse of power by any one organ of the state, and to

TABLE 2.1 India's Political Structure

	Legislature		Executive		Judiciary: Comprising Judges from:		
	Lok Sabha (LS)	Rajya Sabha (RS)	President	Prime Minister (PM) and Council of Ministers	Supreme Court (SC)	High Courts (HC) (presently 24)	Subordinate Courts
Composition	Up to 552 (2 nominated from Anglo Indian community)	Up to 250 (12 nominated)	1	1 for PM; Up to 15% of total number of LS members for Council	Chief Justice of India (CJI) and up to 30 judges	Number of judges vary from state to state and is decided by the president	Civil, criminal, and revenue courts
Qualifications	Citizen of India; at least 25 years old; registered	Citizen of India; at least 30 years old	Citizen of India; at least 35 years old;	Citizen of India; member of either LS or RS;	Citizen of India and any of the following: at least 5 years as	Citizen of India and at least 10 years as judicial	At least 7 years as an advocate or is in the service of

	voter in any Indian constituency	qualified to be elected as LS member	should not be holding office for any other government roles		judge of one or more HC; at least 10 years an advocate of one or more HC; a distinguished jurist according to the president	officer in a district court or below or at least 10 years as an advocate in an HC continuously without break	the state or central government provided he/she possesses required legal qualifications
Appointment	Directly elected through first-past-the-post system	Indirectly elected by state legislatures through proportional	Indirectly elected by electoral college (LS and RS members)	Council of Ministers: by president on the advice of the PM. PM is	By president on recommendation of a collegium consisting	By president on recommendation of a collegium consisting	In most states, judicial officers selected through competitive examination

(*Contd.*)

Table 2.1 (Contd.)

Legislature		Executive		Judiciary: Comprising Judges from:		
Lok Sabha (LS)	Rajya Sabha (RS)	President	Prime Minister (PM) and Council of Ministers	Supreme Court (SC)	High Courts (HC) (presently 24)	Subordinate Courts
	representation (single transferable vote system)	and state legislatures	leader of majority party (or coalition of parties)	of the CJI and four other senior SC judges. By convention, CJI is the most senior judge in the SC	of the CJI and four other senior SC judges. The president consults the CJI and governor of the state before appointing chief justice of an HC	of State Public Service Commission and appointed by Governor in consultation with chief justice of concerned HC

Tenure	5 years (can be dissolved earlier if ruling party loses majority)	Permanent house; one-third members retire every 2 years; members' term is 6 years	5 years	Council of Ministers: Till LS is dissolved or removed by PM	Till the age of 65 years	Till the age of 62 years	Not specified
Functions	Legislative; oversight; financial and representative	Legislative; oversight; and representative	Appoints and removes PM and his council of ministers and judges of SC and HC; assents to bills;	PM heads the government, determines policies of the government (with ministers) and coordinates working	Original jurisdiction: Disputes between Government of India and one or more states; disputes	Original jurisdiction: Hear cases of violation of fundamental rights and issue writs; election petitions Appellate:	Civil: Settle disputes regarding property, contract, divorce, etc., but does not award penalty Criminal: Cases of violation

(*Contd.*)

Table 2.1 (*Contd.*)

Legislature		Executive		Judiciary: Comprising Judges from:		
Lok Sabha (LS)	Rajya Sabha (RS)	President	Prime Minister (PM) and Council of Ministers	Supreme Court (SC)	High Courts (HC) (presently 24)	Subordinate Courts
		approves introduction of money bills and has emergency powers	of the ministries headed by the members of the council of ministers	between two or more states, enforcement of fundamental rights and PILs Appellate: Hears appeals against	Hears appeals against judgments of lower courts Has to confirm death sentence given by lower courts	of law filed by police against an accused. Can award fine, or prison or death sentences Revenue: Relates to revenue on agricultural land in the district

| | | | | judgments of HC Advisory: Can give advice, if sought by the president | | |
| **Removal** | Periodic elections | Periodic elections | Impeachment by Parliament | Council of Ministers: by PM or dissolution of the house | Impeachment by Parliament | Impeachment by Parliament | By state government in consultation with the HC |

Sources: Constitution of India (http://lawmin.nic.in/olwing/cci/coi-english/coi-indexenglish.htm), Lok Sabha and Rajya Sabha websites (loksabha.gov.in and rajyasabha.gov.in); online curriculum of NIOS (http://www.nios.ac.in/online-course-material/sr-secondary-courses/political-science-(317)/english-medium.aspx).

ensure a rule of law rather than a rule based on the whims of an individual or group. However, opting for the Westminster (British) model over the presidential system meant that there was overlap between the legislature and the executive (the council of ministers was a subset of the members of Parliament [MPs]). The separation of the executive and judiciary was followed more carefully.

Fundamental Rights and Directive Principles

Articles 14–32 of Part III of the Constitution of India enumerate the fundamental rights—equality before law; freedom of speech and expression; life and liberty; religion and culture; constitutional remedies against exploitation. These rights are justiciable, that is, judiciary has to enforce them. The legislature and the executive cannot curb these rights either by law or by an executive order. The Supreme Court or the High Courts can set aside any law found to be infringing or abridging the Fundamental Rights. In recent years, the courts have interpreted the right to life in order to push the executive to bring forth a rights-based legislation, such as Right to Education (RTE) and Right to Food Security.

In order to ensure socio-economic justice through a welfare state, the Constitution lays down desirable principles in Part IV, known as Directive Principles of State Policy. They include a variety of pointers to state policy ranging from Panchayati Raj to uniform civil code, environmental protection, improved nutrition, and education. Though non-justiciable, they provide legitimacy and support to aligned advocacy groups in the fight for their causes.

Local Self-governance

The 73rd and 74th Constitutional Amendments of 1992 added a third layer to the Indian federal structure—the rural and urban local bodies, panchayats, and municipalities. The amendments made statutory provisions for the establishment and functioning of urban and rural local self-governing institutions. However, the states can decide the extent of devolution and control the purse strings.

Schedule 12 of the Constitution enumerates the subjects that fall within the jurisdiction of the local governments which includes urban planning, water supply, roads and bridges, slum improvement, and regulation of land use. However, local self-government continues to be in the state list, thus allowing the states to decide on the extent of devolution of powers. Devolution of powers varies significantly across states, and over the years, it has been far more effective for the rural (panchayat) side than the urban (municipality) side.

Stages of Policy Formulation

The Identification Stage (Agenda-setting)

The first critical step in the policy formulation process is 'agenda-setting', that is, determining what is to be decided. To get on the agenda, problems must first come to the notice of the policymakers. Putting an issue on the 'agenda' of policymakers can be a long and arduous process, and can be done in the following different ways: (a) sustained public campaigns by activists; (b) a crisis leading to public outcry for the government to act on an issue; (c) using a 'trigger' or 'focus event(s)' to launch a campaign; and (d) pro-active action from the government in response to the needs of administrators.

When Mohini Jain, a young student from Meerut, approached the Supreme Court in 1991 for relief against the high fees being charged by a private medical college in Karnataka, little did she know the impact it would have on the education sector. For the first time in 1992, the court declared that 'the right to education is concomitant to fundamental rights enshrined under Part III of the Constitution', and 'every citizen has a right to education under the Constitution' (*Mohini Jain* v. *State of Karnataka* (1992) SCR (3) 658). The RTE was then reinforced in the *Unnikrishnan* case of 1993, although the court restricted it for children up to 14 years of age (*Unnikrishnan J.P.* v. *State of Andhra Pradesh* (1993) SCR (1) 594).

This ruling, though crucial, was not enough to get the attention of the policymakers about the state of education in the country. It took a large number of dedicated activists to give visibility to the issue and bring it on the agenda of the policymakers. Building on the Campaign Against Child Labour, launched in 1992 as a network of organizations working against child labour, a number of activists working in different NGOs such as Pratham, MV Foundation, Child Rights and You (or simply CRY), and Eklavya used the Supreme Court judgment to galvanize activists across the country into a spirited campaign for RTE (Narayan 2005). A postcard campaign called Voice of India was launched where grassroots NGOs across the country mobilized people to send a postcard to the president, emphasizing on making RTE a reality. The success of this campaign led to the formation of the National Alliance for the Fundamental Right to Education (NAFRE), a coalition of pro-education NGOs across the country. These NGOs, under the overall leadership of NAFRE, then mobilized support for the RTE among the grassroots, organized rallies and sit-ins, and advocated with policymakers for the RTE to be made a fundamental right. Their efforts bore fruit in 2002 in the form of a constitutional amendment.

The judicial order (*Unnikrishnan* case of 1993) provided the impetus for turning education from a virtual non-issue to a fundamental right. But even having education as a fundamental right did not give effective 'bite'. It needed yet another sustained campaign over the next seven years to finally enact the RTE legislation in 2009.

As the above example shows, problems can be identified and put on the agenda of policymakers through sustained advocacy by civil society organizations. They can alert the government towards the need for a particular legislation or change in an existing law. Civil society campaigns employ a range of methods of varying shrillness to mobilize public support for their cause and in turn pressurize legislators to enact laws. Lobbying, rallies, sit-ins, dharnas, hunger strikes, post-card campaigns, internet campaigns, *jan-sunwai*s (public hearings), conferences and seminars, public interest litigations (PIL), signature campaigns, television interviews, newspapers articles, and social media campaigns are all part of commonly used tactics to campaign for policy change.

The presence of skilled policy activists or policy entrepreneurs makes a big difference in ensuring that a particular issue gets on to the policy agenda out of countless others in what John Kingdon (1995) calls the 'primeval soup'.

Sometimes a crisis or 'focusing event' helps to bring a problem to light. For example, in December 2012, a young physiotherapy student, returning home with her friend after a movie, was brutally raped by five men in the heart of Delhi and left to die by the roadside. This incident (commonly referred to as the 'Nirbhaya' rape case) touched a chord among the middle-class youth leading to a huge public outcry against the lack of women's safety in the country and the ineffectiveness of rape laws. The intensity of the protests that followed for almost a month forced the government to first set up a commission to recommend changes to the rape laws, and then amend the laws in Parliament, all within a period of three months.

For activists, the timing of their campaigns is very important to grab the attention of the public and policymakers. A large part of the success of the Jan Lokpal (translated as Citizen's Ombudsman) campaign of 2011, spearheaded by Arvind Kejriwal, the current CM of Delhi, was because of apt timing. A number of big-ticket scams had come to light during 2009–10 (2G scam, CWG scam, coal-block scam). Corruption seemed like the biggest barrier to India's prosperity with no solution in sight. In this scenario, Kejriwal's 'India Against Corruption' movement came as a breath of fresh air. The clever involvement of Anna Hazare, an octogenarian social activist with an impeccable reputation, as a symbol of the movement helped galvanize the largely middle-class public to support the demand for setting up an independent anti-corruption body to investigate corruption cases. The 24×7 media coverage of Hazare's repeated fasts and the groundswell of public support forced the government to take cognizance of the issue.

The government can suo moto decide that a law or policy is required in a particular sector. It may get inputs from specialized bodies, such as the National Human Rights Commission and the Law Commission, or appoint a group to study a sector and draft a law or policy. These groups or bodies may hold consultations with independent experts and stakeholders. Take the case of financial sector legislation. In March 2011, the government set up the Financial Sector Legislative Reforms Commission, under the leadership of Justice (Retd) B.N. Srikrishna to comprehensively review and redraw legislations governing India's financial system. The report, submitted in 2013, is the roadmap for many of the financial sector reforms the government introduced thereafter.

The major actors in the policy-formulation process include advocacy groups, NGOs, lobby groups, media, judiciary, and think tanks. Interest or pressure groups represent a particular section and push for getting some benefit for it. They primarily use one-to-one lobbying with policymakers. Many business conglomerates fund the national and state-level election campaigns. Big farmers also exert influence on the policy agenda through lobbying. Less powerful groups such as Dalit groups, women's rights groups, and environmental activists use collective advocacy and mass mobilization (the power of numbers) to influence policy agendas. They present perspectives and knowledge from their own work in seminars and conferences and conduct independent evaluation of existing policies. They file PILs in the judiciary; and sometimes collaborate with think tanks to gather evidence.

Media plays a crucial role by shaping the context in which policies are drafted. They build public opinion through analysis and discussions. India has over 80,000 registered national and regional newspapers and over 400 television news channels in English and regional languages. Media coverage of protests played a crucial role in publicising the Jan Lokpal campaign as well as the protests after the Nirbhaya rape case.

The Articulation Stage (Drafting)

As activists lobbied parliamentarians for the fundamental RTE, some MPs took an active interest and started their own parliamentary forum on children. The bureaucracy held consultations with concerned stakeholders and a bill was introduced in Parliament in 2001 to amend the Constitution (the Constitution (93rd Amendment) Bill, 2001). The bill was enacted in 2002 (as the Constitution (86th Amendment) Act, 2002) but a law was needed to operationalize the fundamental right on the ground.

The second phase of civil society activism for the RTE Act took place between 2002 and 2009 when the government finally introduced a bill in Parliament in 2009. The bill went through a series of iterations before it was tabled in the house.

Box 2.1 lists the stages involved in the drafting of a bill. The formal drafting of the law takes place at this stage, primarily within the ministries by the concerned bureaucrats. Although not mandatory by law, the ministries hold formal and informal consultations with experts, activists, interest groups, and other

Box 2.1 Process of Bill Drafting

The concerned ministry drafts the government bills, which are then vetted by other ministries. The process usually has the following stages:

(a) The domain department decides the legislative intent, which is shared with the law department.

(b) The law department gives its inputs mostly on the constitutional validity and permissibility of the proposals.

(c) The domain department prepares the first draft of the law. If it is by a law-enforcing department, the inputs of the litigation cell are also necessary.

(d) This draft goes to the legislative department which uses its experience with similar and related laws to come up with a second draft. This can take six to ten months.

(e) The revised draft is referred first to the internal committee of the department of legislative affairs. Then it goes to the department of legal affairs which examines, clause by clause, the constitutional validity.

(f) The cabinet secretariat then examines it and presents it to the cabinet.

(g) Major laws are typically referred to a group of ministers.

stakeholders. In fact, in 2014, the central government introduced a policy on pre-legislative consultation to be followed by every ministry before submitting a legislative proposal (including subordinate legislation) to the Ministry of Law and Justice for vetting. (Ministry of Law and Justice 2014.)

The policy mandates that a draft bill is placed in the public domain for 30 days: this should include a justification for its introduction, financial implications, estimated impact assessment, and an explanatory note for key legal provisions. The draft bill would then be referred to the Ministry of Law and Justice for vetting (the process of inter-ministerial consultations also has to be conducted before referring the bill to the Law Ministry).

It is common for the government to approach an independent expert to provide a report before drafting a major law. For example, the Ministry of Finance had appointed the Bankruptcy Law Reforms Committee under the leadership of Dr T.K. Vishwanathan on 22 August 2014 to study the corporate bankruptcy legal framework in India. The committee submitted its report on 4 November 2015. Based on the report, the Insolvency and Bankruptcy Code, 2015, was introduced in the Lok Sabha on 21 December 2015. This was passed on 5 May 2016 by the Lok Sabha and on 11 May 2016 by the Rajya Sabha.

Drafting policies or legislations is no easy task and policymakers have to work under many constraints—economic, political, socio-cultural, and international. Resources have to be allocated optimally, trade-offs have to be considered, short-term and long-term policy impacts have to be measured, and coalition members as well as the opposition have to be managed (especially if the same party is not in the majority in both houses). Should a law to regulate the microfinance industry cap the interest rates that microfinance institutions (MFI) can charge? Would it be in the long-term interest of the borrower since it would impact the growth of the industry? Should the rights of tribals to forest land be prioritized over the need to protect animal habitats? Should we opt for a targeted food security scheme over a universal scheme? Would cash transfer be more efficient than a public distribution system in helping the poor?

Key actors at this stage are the bureaucracy, activists, independent experts, committees and councils, and legislators. The bureaucracy is the executive arm of the government. It not only guides the process of policy formation but is also responsible for its implementation after the policy is adopted by the legislature. The bureaucracy advises ministers on policy matters as the ministers themselves may lack technical knowledge of the subject. Experts working in think tanks, legal firms, and/or academia play a vital role as informants on policy issues. They develop policy ideas as well as evaluate the effectiveness and functionality of existing policies. There are many instances of the government consulting with experts. For example, the Companies Law Committee, set up in 2016 to review the Companies Act, 2013, included members of Institute of Cost Accountants of India (ICMAI), Institute of Chartered Accountants of India (ICAI), and Federation of Indian Chambers of Commerce and Industry (FICCI).

The Planning Commission, until recently, played a crucial role in the policy formulation stage. As a government think tank and fund allocator between the centre and the states, it was charged with the responsibility of assessing all resources in the country and formulating plans for the most effective and balanced utilization of resources and determining priorities. In January 2015, the Narendra Modi government replaced the Planning Commission with the NITI Aayog. The stated aim of the NITI Aayog is to foster participation of state governments in the policymaking process. As a demonstration of this aim, in February 2015, Prime Minister Modi set up three sub-groups of CMs for making recommendations in the areas of centrally sponsored schemes, skill development, and Swachh Bharat Abhiyan.

During the two terms of the United Progressive Alliance (UPA) (2004–14), in order to oversee the implementation of the Common Minimum Programme, the central government appointed the National Advisory Council (NAC), a body comprising professionals in diverse fields of development activity who served in their individual capacities. They also acted as an interface between the government and civil society in the discussion on a variety of legislations including the access to information law, the MNREGA, and the food security law.

The Policy Adoption Stage

The formal adoption of a law takes place when members of each house of Parliament debate and then vote on the bill. A simple majority is sufficient for ordinary bills; for constitutional amendment, a two-thirds majority of the members present and voting in the house is required. Box 2.2 lists the major steps in the passage of a bill once it has been introduced in Parliament.

The speed with which the bills get enacted varies considerably. If policy change comes about through incremental steps, some serious lasting mistakes may be avoided. However, it may also mean that the system is not efficient enough to deal with a perceived problem in a time-bound manner. Table 2.2 shows that the government has been responsive in some cases, especially where an external event has provided a trigger for change such as the Lokpal and Lokayuktas Act, 2013 (although the pace slowed once the momentum of the India against Corruption movement died down) and the Criminal Law (Amendment) Act, 2013.

Key actors at this stage are the legislators, political parties, council of ministers, standing committees, state governments, bureaucracy, and independent regulators. The role of non-state actors is confined to making representations to the concerned standing committee or a political party. Political parties and legislators play

Box 2.2   Passage of Bills in Parliament

1. A bill can be introduced either in the Lok Sabha or the Rajya Sabha (except money bills which can only be introduced in the Lok Sabha). This stage is known as the *first reading*. At this stage, MPs can oppose the introduction of a bill and the matter may be put to a vote in the house. For instance, in August 2009, the law minister withdrew the motion to introduce the Judges (Disclosure of Assets and Liabilities) Bill as several MPs were opposed to the bill on grounds that it violated the Constitution.

2. After a bill has been introduced, the presiding officer of the concerned house (the Speaker in case of the Lok Sabha, the Chair in case of Rajya Sabha) may refer the bill to the concerned Departmentally Related Standing Committee (DRSCs) for examination. Generally, most bills are referred to these DRSCs, however, the presiding officer of the house has the discretion not to do so. For instance, key bills such as the Special Economic Zones Bill, 2005 and the National Investigation Agency Bill, 2008 were not referred to a DRSC. In contrast, the Rajya Sabha sent the Lokpal Bill passed by the Lok Sabha to a select committee although it had already been examined by the DRSC. These

DRSCs may solicit feedback from the public by issuing notices in key newspapers and the Gazette of India. The public comments are also tabled in the form of a report.

3. The Standing Committee considers the broad objectives and the specific clauses of the bill referred to it and may invite public comments on a bill. Bills which come under the ambit of a number of different ministries, may be referred to a joint committee. The committee then submits its recommendations in the form of a report to parliament. The government is, however, not bound to accept the recommendations of the DRSC.

4. In the *second reading* (consideration), the bill is scrutinized thoroughly. Each clause of the bill is discussed on the floor of the house and it may be accepted, amended, or rejected.

5. During the *third reading* (passing), the house votes on the redrafted bill.

6. If the bill is passed in one house, it is then sent to the other house, where it goes through second and third readings. During the second reading, the government, or any MP, may introduce amendments to the bill, some of which may be based on recommendations of the Standing Committee.

(*Contd.*)

Box 2.2 (*Contd.*)

7. After both houses of parliament pass a bill, it is presented to the president for assent. He/she has the right to seek information and clarification about the bill, and may return it to Parliament for reconsideration. (This may be done only once. If both houses pass the bill again, the president has to give assent.)

8. After the president gives assent, the bill is notified as an act and brought into force.

a crucial role during the legislative process. The stand taken by a legislator on a bill primarily depends on his/her party affiliation. The party leaders decide what stand to take on a bill and members have to conform, especially if a whip is issued. The Anti-Defection law of 1984 defines defection as, among other things, voting against a party whip. The violation of a party whip can invite expulsion. At this time, ministers and opposition members negotiate and bargain to gain political concessions with each other. Trinamool Congress leader, Mamata Banerjee, used such tactics in 2012 to arm-twist the UPA government in giving her financial concessions in return for her support for

TABLE 2.2 Timelines of the Select Laws and Bills

Act/Bill	Pre-legislative	Legislative
The Competition Act, 2002	11 years	1 year, 4 months
The Right to Information Act, 2005	15 years	5 months
The Right of Children to Free and Compulsory Education, 2009	16 years	Constitutional Amendment Act: 1 year RTE Act: 8 months
The Child Labour (Prohibition and Regulation) Amendment Bill, 2012	25 years	Not passed. Introduction to Standing Committee Report: 1 year
The Microfinance Institutions (Development and Regulation) Bill, 2012	14 years	Not passed. Introduction to Standing Committee Report: 1 year, 9 months
The National Food Security Act, 2013	21 years	1 year, 9 months
The Lokpal and Lokayuktas Act, 2013	3 years	2 years, 4 months
The Right to Fair Compensation and Transparency in Land Acquisition, Rehabilitation and Resettlement Act, 2013	17 years	2 years
The Criminal Law (Amendment) Act, 2013	3 months	1 month

Source: Lok Sabha and Rajya Sabha websites and authors' own research.

passing the budget. The relevant standing committees generally consult state governments since most bills are implemented at the state level.

The 24 DRSCs also play a crucial role at this stage. These committees, introduced in 1993, ensure oversight on each ministry. Given the volume of work and the limited time at their disposal, legislators were unable to scrutinize every matter in detail on the floor of the house. Some of this work is now entrusted to committees, which are composed of groups of MPs. These committees review proposed laws, inspect activities of the executive branch, and scrutinize government expenditure. Their reports allow for informed debate in Parliament. Committees also provide a forum to build consensus across party lines, help develop expertise in subjects, and enable consultation with independent experts and stakeholders. Each DRSC has 31 members, 21 from Lok Sabha and 10 from Rajya Sabha. Seats on each committee are allocated to parties in proportion to their strength in the house. The chair of a committee is appointed by the speaker or chairperson of the relevant house.

After a bill is passed, it needs to get the assent of the president to become a law. However, even that is not adequate for it to move to the implementation stage. It needs to be notified in the Gazette of India, a step that can be held up for up to several months or years in some cases (the Delhi Rent Act, passed in 1995 was never notified until its repeal in 2013). Even after notification, the readiness for implementation has to await the 'rules' for the act developed by the relevant ministry and tabled in Parliament though rarely discussed. In many cases, the rule-making process can hold up operationalization of laws by multiple years (the Food Safety and Standards Act was enacted in 2006 but its rules did not come until 2011).

Apart from legislative acts, policy is also formulated through the rulings of independent regulators that have gained in importance since India liberalized its economy in the 1990s allowing the private sector to operate in areas which were earlier government monopolies such as in electricity, telecommunications, insurance, securities market, and oil and gas. While regulators have independence in performing their role, they still fall within the broad definition of the executive branch of the State, and are accountable to the legislature. There is some confusion about this though. For instance in the US, the chairman of the

Federal Reserve regularly deposes before the Senate Committee on Finance, but in India, the Reserve Bank of India (RBI), while notionally independent, is not currently required to do so.

Regulators have the power to formulate policies and ensure its adherence. Policymakers find significant advantages in governance through a regulator. Neither does it generally share the 'social' obligations of the government, nor is it expected to be affected by the pressures of 'interest' groups. It can provide a level playing field to all participants without fear or favour. It can build expertise matching the complexities of the task and evolves processes to enforce authority rapidly and proactively. It is better placed than the government to take unpopular, but necessary, decisions.

Moving Ahead

This chapter outlined the broad processes of policy formulation in three stages—agenda setting, articulation, and adoption. These guidelines, nevertheless, permit significant variation across cases of policy formulation, and the actual formulation of policy is determined by the contemporary pulls and pushes of politics. The extent to which the theoretical frameworks discussed at the beginning of the chapter, all framed largely in western contexts, are useful for understanding India's policy formulation scenario is an interesting topic for research.

Over time, policy formulation has undeniably shifted from secret confabulations of the powerful few to a more transparent, participative process. Nevertheless, the interaction and power play among various stakeholders in policy formulation need to be understood better. Policy research is only beginning to lift the lid here.

Formulation is the first of the three major steps of policymaking. However, even the most ideally formulated policy would be toothless without effective implementation. This is the subject matter of the next chapter.

3

Policy Implementation
Framework and Challenges

The National Health Insurance Scheme—Rashtriya Swasthya Bima Yojana (RSBY)—aims to improve poor people's access to quality healthcare.... Six months after initiation in early 2010, an impressive 85% of eligible households in the sample were aware of the scheme, and 68% had been enrolled. However, the scheme was hardly operational and utilisation was virtually zero. A large proportion of beneficiaries were yet to receive their cards, and many did not know how and where to obtain treatment under the scheme. Moreover, hospitals were not ready to treat RSBY patients. Surveyed hospitals complained of a lack of training and delays in the reimbursement of their expenses. Many were refusing to treat patients until the issues were resolved, and others were asking cardholders to pay cash. As is typical for the implementation of a government scheme, many of the problems can be related to a misalignment of incentives.

—Rajasekhar et al. (2011)

The above description could apply to a vast number of programmes and policies in India (as well as, to be fair, in several other countries) over decades, cutting across states, political dispensations in authority, and nature of the programme or the ministry involved. Yet, a brilliantly formulated policy, which is not implemented effectively, is undoubtedly an exercise in vain. It is easy to find fault with the implementation record of the various national and state governments. However, an attempt to improve implementation must involve an effort to find the root causes of poor implementation and to avoid them or make provisions for them in the design stage. The questions to ask then, should include the following:

1. What are the typical factors that make for poor implementation of a policy?

2. Are our policies implementable or just noble? Do we formulate policies keeping the implementing mechanism and reality in mind?

3. Can the flaws in the implementing structure be fixed?

4. Should policy delivery be the responsibility only of the government or should non-governmental entities, beneficiaries, and stakeholders stay involved?

5. Are there lessons to be learnt from administrations that are generally believed to have done a better job of policy implementation?

Before attempting to answer any of these questions, it is important to begin by briefly describing the policy implementation mechanism in India. Policy implementation is the job of the executive branch of government, which means there are one or more relevant ministries for a particular policy or a programme. The federal structure of the Indian government is also a key aspect here. With the exception of a few key union subjects like finance, foreign affairs, and defence, most matters of public policy that actually affect the day-to-day lives of citizens are implemented at the state level. It is done through the combined agency of the relevant state ministry (which may set up a specialized agency to deliver the programme) and the district- and block-level bureaucracies (the district magistrate or block development officers, who are responsible for the execution of the programme in their respective domain). The 'last mile', depending upon the nature of the programme, may involve a network of government employees like school teachers, post office workers, or a set of individuals specially recruited for the programme (see Table 3.1 for a structure of the administrative machinery).

The structure presented in Table 3.1 is a highly stylized one. District administration in particular involves many more officers and staff, and the organization structure vary across districts. Without going into too much detail, Figure 3.1, with Panel A depicting the organization charts of Devanagare district in Karnataka and Panel B depicting that of Kullu district in Himachal Pradesh, gives a sense of the roles and departments involved and the range of variations.

This section portrays a user's perspective of a large national programme. The next section looks at the

TABLE 3.1 Structure of the Administrative Machinery at Centre, State, and District Levels—A Stylized Overview

Structure	Centre			State		District	Sub-district
	Central Secretariat (Central Ministries)	Cabinet Secretariat	Prime Minister's Office	State Secretariat	Directorate	Collectorate	Sub-division, Tehsil, Blocks, Village
Composition	Includes all ministries; political head: minister; administrative head: secretary	Political head: prime minister (PM); administrative head: cabinet secretary	Political head: PM; administrative head: principal secretary	Political head of state: chief minister (CM); administrative head of state: chief secretary, ministries, and departments;	Head of the directorate	District collector/deputy commissioner	SDO-SDM/ assistant collector, tehsildar, block development officer, patwari

			political head: minister; administrative head: secretary				
Functions	Assist ministers in making and modifying policies, legislation, rules and regulations; budgeting; sectoral planning; oversight of policy execution and evaluation	Provide secretarial assistance to the cabinet and its committees; provide information; keep records of discussions, act as coordinating agency	Deals with all government files in the office and apprises the PM of important documents; looks after affairs of different ministries on directions from the PM;	Chief secretary: principal advisor to CM, secretary to state cabinet, and chief co-ordinator of state administration. State secretariat: assist minister, formulate policies and	Provide technical advice to ministers, prepare budget, inspect implementation of work by department staff; advice state service commissions on promotions and	Revenue, maintenance of law and order, coordinator of different departments, crisis management, development functions, conducts census, returning officer	SDO: Revenue and law and order tehsildar: land revenue, land records, general administration BDO: development

(*Contd.*)

Table 3.1 (Contd.)

Structure	Centre			State		District	Sub-district
	Central Secretariat (Central Ministries)	Cabinet Secretariat	Prime Minister's Office	State Secretariat	Directorate	Collectorate	Sub-division, Tehsil, Blocks, Village
	of results; coordinating with state governments and parliamentary responsibilities	among ministries	coordinates activities of various personnel in the office; liaises with ministries and state governments	programmes of state government, coordinate among the programmes, prepare budget, frame laws, review implementation	organize in-service training	during elections	management and management of panchayat samiti

Sources: NIOS curriculum, as available at http://download.nos.org/srsec317newE/317EL34.pdf, last accessed on 15 February 2016.

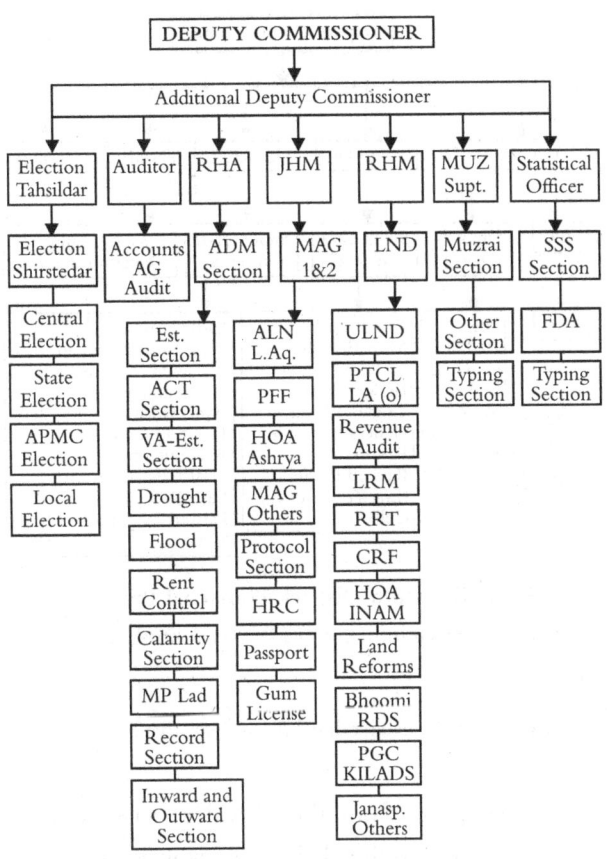

Panel A: Davanagare District, Karnataka

Source: http://davanagere.nic.in/DCOFFICE/administra-tion.html, last accessed on 15 February 2016.

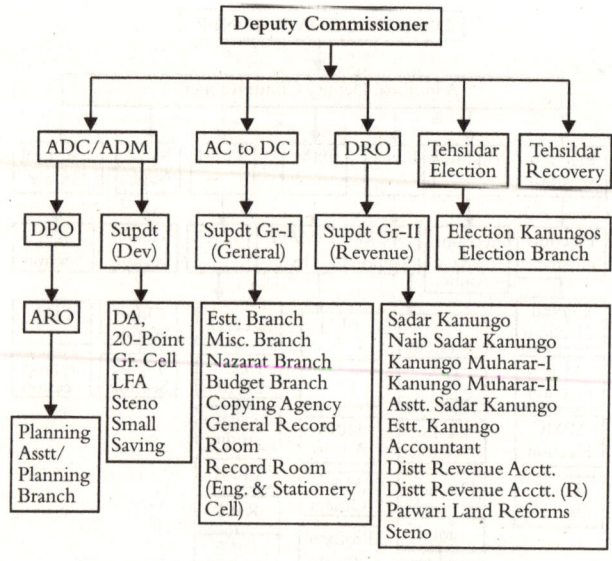

Panel B: Kullu District, Himachal Pradesh
Source: http://hpkullu.nic.in/RTIVDD-1.html, last accessed on 15 February 2016.

FIGURE 3.1 District-level Administrative Structures

same programme from the provider's viewpoint in order to appreciate the challenges involved. The third section analyses several constraints that plague the Indian state in adequately implementing programmes. The fourth section covers a few broad management principles relevant for policy implementation, and the fifth section presents a case study of a successful policy implementation strategy at the state level—that of the first term of the National Democratic Alliance (NDA) government in Bihar in 2005–10.

Implementation Challenges: Scale and Coordination across Agencies

As a centrally sponsored scheme, RSBY is designed, funded, and monitored by the union government (initially under the Ministry of Labour and Employment, later shifted to Ministry of Health and Family Welfare in 2015) but its actual nation-wide roll-out happens through the state governments (respective ministries of health). Box 3.1 summarizes the broad steps involved.

Delivering a developmental programme to people is not a simple affair. For a national programme, it frequently involves a workforce of thousands and a clientele of tens, if not hundreds, of millions. It also requires anticipating abuse and plugging gaps through which unscrupulous elements can exploit the system (the RSBY has had its share of allegations of doctors and patients colluding to produce fictitious or

Box 3.1

Implementing the RSBY involves a set of complex and interrelated activities broadly given as follows:

Selection of Insurance Agencies

State governments, through a competitive public bidding process, select a public or private insurance company. Each contract is specified on the basis of an individual district in a state and the insurer agrees to set up an office in each district.

Hospital Empanelment

After the insurance company is selected, the state governments need to empanel both public and private healthcare providers in the project and nearby districts. These hospitals should install necessary hardware and software so that smart card transactions can be processed and set up a special RSBY desk with a trained staff. The insurer must also provide a list of RSBY empanelled hospitals, to the beneficiaries at the time of enrolment. When empanelment takes place, a national unique hospital ID number is generated so that transactions can be tracked at each hospital.

Preparation of Beneficiary Data

RSBY provides health insurance for the enrolled BPL and other defined category of families from each district.

Respective state governments need to convert their existing beneficiary data in electronic format for each district and send these data to the central government, which in turn checks the compatibility of this data with the standard format and allocates a Unique Reference Number (URN) for each family.

Enrolment Process

The selected insurance company then downloads the URN data. The company prepares enrolment plan in consultation with district authorities and enrols the listed families at village-level enrolment camps. At enrolment stations, photographs and fingerprints are captured using the enrolment kit, and smartcards are printed and handed over to the family after collecting registration fee of Rs 30 per card.

How Services Are Availed by the Beneficiary

The transaction process begins when the beneficiary visits the participating hospital. The RSBY helpdesk at the hospital verifies the identity of the beneficiary by his/her photograph and fingerprints, which are stored on his/her smart card. In case of hospitalization, approved services are paid for using the card.

(*Contd.*)

Box 3.1 (*Contd.*)

Claim Settlements

After the patient has been treated, the hospitals need to send an electronic hospitalization and claims data to the insurer/third party administrator (TPA). A copy of this data is transferred simultaneously to the server of the government. This has to be done within the 24 hours. Any delay beyond this stipulated period and up to 30 days of transaction will have to be explained by the concerned hospital. The insurer/TPA after going through the records information will make the payment to the hospital within a month of the receipt of claims.

Financing of the Scheme

The fund-sharing pattern between the central and state governments is 75:25. The beneficiary has to pay a fee of Rs 30 every year at the time of enrolment.

Grievance Redressal Management

If any stakeholder has a grievance in connection with the validity, interpretation, implementation, or alleged breach of any provision of the scheme, it will be settled by the relevant grievance committee at the district, state, and national levels.

Source: Summarized from http://www.rsby.gov.in/how_works.aspx. Original language largely retained.

worse, unnecessary procedures). Finally, avoiding any appearance of impropriety is critical, to escape possible harassment in the hands of what is often referred to as the 'C³I'—the Central Bureau of Investigation (CBI), Comptroller and Auditor General (CAG), Central Vigilance Commission (CVC), and the Right to Information (RTI). Critics often point to private sector efficiency, but the private sector rarely undertakes any rollout in scales that governments do, and certainly not in the timelines or on the budgets involved.

Herein lies the implementation challenge. The field of implementation is also changing fast with quick adoption of IT technology and the internet by the government. E-governance is visualized to be a game changer for public service delivery.

The Capability Constraint

There are at least four elements that arguably inhibit the delivery capability of the Indian state when it comes to public services:

1. The sheer number of dispensers of public services per capita is very small;

2. The recruitment process of public servants does not insist upon their skills for the role they need to play;

3. The initial as well as mid-career training is not adequate to prepare the public servants for their role; and

4. The incentives of individual bureaucrats are not in place to motivate them for their role.

Let us look at these four elements sequentially. In 2013, India had 130 police officers for every 100,000 citizens. For the US, in 2008, the number was 348. Among the 50 countries ranked in 2010 on this metric by the United Nations Office on Drugs and Crime (UNODC), India came in second from the bottom, ahead only of Uganda. India has only 15 judges per million people while the corresponding figures for other countries are: US 108, France 109, and UK 35 (Jain 2014). The total number of the elite IAS (Indian Administrative Services) officers serving in February 2016 is 5,196. This group has to operate the administration in more than 683 districts in the country, the governments of 29 states and 7 union territories in addition to the multi-tiered ministries of the central government. In 2013, India had a diplomatic corps strength of 930, just ahead of the city-state of Singapore at 867, dwarfed by China at 4,000 not to speak of the US's 20,000 (Mohan 2013). Broadly speaking, the number of 'tax employees' or government personnel per 1,000 people stood at 0.006 in India as opposed to 1.6 for UK, 0.04 for Brazil, and 0.03 for Turkey (Kapur 2012).

More than a little of this workforce shortage is the artefact of the recruiting system possibly made difficult by reservations. At the end of 2010, for instance, nearly a quarter of the police posts (0.5 million out of 2.1 million) lay vacant. More than 0.4 million people took the civil services examination in 2009, which had 989 posts vacant, a staggering 875 persons per vacancy. Yet, the UPSC could only recommend 875 persons, or 0.88 per vacancy! Moreover, it is not only the civil services alone that have such high standards. The applicant to post ratio and the recommended to post ratio stood at 260 and 0.87, respectively, for that year's Engineering Services Examination, 164 and 0.87 respectively for the central police services (assistant commandants) examination, 101 and 0.65 for the Indian Economic Service/Indian Statistical Service examination, 13 and 0.76 for geologists' examination, 84 and 0.89 for combined medical services examination of 2010.

If recruiting is a challenge, then retention is not simple either. With the private sector booming since liberalization, exits from the government to the private sector have become increasingly frequent. With lateral entry being a rare exception, and strict service rules and bureaucratic delays adding to the problem, a large number of key government posts remain unfilled. In 2012, as many as 3,400 civil service posts—with 1,777 Indian Administrative Service (IAS) and 1,255 Indian Police Service (IPS) posts—were vacant, thus affecting the speed of decision-making.

The suitability of candidates is an equally problematic area. The union and state civil services examinations have been modelled on the Indian Civil Services system that started in 1893 (which, in turn, was modelled after the staffing structure of the East India Company) in an era pre-dating the birth of management or public policy as fields of study. Also, it was a system meant to keep a nation under the thumb of an alien power. The emphasis on general education, with subjects that have little to do with actual

nature of the bureaucrats' work, has unfortunately continued. Aptitude tests are yet to make their way into
the recruiting system. As a result, the people selected,
while undoubtedly bright, are not necessarily the best
fit for the role.

Appropriate training could solve the problem
to some extent, but that too remains a challenging task for a service that has to serve myriad roles
in a vastly diverse nation. At the end of the day, the
bureaucracy, by its recruitment, training, and on-the-
job learning in district administration roles, creates
legions of generalists largely apt in general administration but not particularly deep in its understanding of increasingly complex issues, processes, and
practices.

The career progression of a person also creates its
challenges. An officer spends the first decade and a
half in district administration, moving to policymaking at the state capital, and possibly on deputation to
the centre, taking on a wide variety of roles that vary
possibly from finance to defence to rural development
to science and technology. The policies he/she helps
shape need to be implementable by the juniors at the
district levels.

As new policies keep being added to the list, the last-mile responsibility of delivery typically gets piled on the district magistrate's shoulders, making him/her responsible for an increasing variety of functions. As collector he/she is responsible of collection of land revenue and myriad other taxes as well as land acquisition issues, if any; as district magistrate, of general law and order; and as development officer he/she is the nodal head of all developmental programmes in the district as well as the Panchayati Raj system. He/she also serves a wide retinue of miscellaneous services like from being the chief returning officer, and census officer of the district to ensuring protocol and performing ceremonial functions. The most industrious and devoted of individuals cannot do justice to all the roles assigned to this position.

The Incentive/Motivation Challenge

The next challenge in implementation is of incentives and resulting motivation. The government's incentive system is infamous for its emphasis on seniority and marginal recognition of performance. In recent years, the government has sought to remedy the situation through the institution of prime minister's awards in the category of governance and e-governance to recognize outstanding and innovative performance by officers. Moreover, in terms of career progress, an officer is typically assessed through an annual report written by his/her direct superior. Given the importance of seniority in personnel decisions and often the short tenure in a particular role coupled with job security, the incentive for policy implementers to go the extra mile is indeed rather limited. Nevertheless, it is not difficult to find government officers working 10–12 hours a day and on weekends to cope with the workload.

However, not all officers are that conscientious, and the opportunities of graft at all levels of the hierarchy—from ministers to lowest functionaries—are often exploited by a large enough section of officers adversely affecting the quality of policy implementation. Corruption by government functionaries is exclusive neither to India nor to the modern era. Kautilya (as cited in Basu 2015) had famously observed over two millennia ago: 'Just as it is impossible to know when a fish moving in water is drinking it, so it is impossible to find out when government servants in charge of undertakings misappropriate money.' However, while corruption exists in varying degrees in all countries and dominantly, though not exclusively, in the public sector, trouble begins when its scale reaches a point where the policy initiatives are rendered useless through leakages in the system. Rajiv Gandhi's famous statement in 1985 put the scale of India's leakages at 85 per cent of the government spending (no one is exactly sure where he came up with that figure from, but it is probably okay to give him the benefit of doubt on this instance).

Attempts at prevention of this unfortunate malaise has created multiple institutions—government organizations like the CBI (whose senior officers, ironically, have also been charged with graft), CVC, CAG, and of late the RTI. These institutions, while undoubtedly much-needed, also require honest bureaucrats to create a paper trail so that vested interests or personal rivalry cannot implicate them later in false charges. The case of the former coal secretary, P.C. Parakh, reputed for his integrity, who was arrested over the coal scam investigation by CBI, provides an apt instance. Such instances further hamstring policy implementation.

Not all neglect of implementation is because of corruption though. Deep-rooted subconscious biases are often at play. Consider the following observation from noted economist and activist, Jean Drèze (2002: 818):

> Campaigning activities in Rajasthan gave me plenty of opportunities to observe the deep hostility of the government bureaucracy towards the poor. There are, of course, sympathetic and dedicated individuals at all levels of the bureaucracy. But the overall mind-set in these circles strikes me as extremely anti-poor. One manifestation of this is the pervasive tendency to blame the victims for their own predicament. Poor people are blamed for being lazy, for not sending their children to school, for squandering their money on drink, and so on. In the context of drought relief, they were constantly accused (against all evidence) of being unwilling to take up employment on relief works. Now, this hostility appears to me to be an objective feature of the work culture in government offices.

While one can debate the degree, universality, and accuracy of the stereotypes mentioned above, it is undeniable that the rulers and the ruled in India come from very different realities. The bureaucracy—and not just the elite services, but even the lowest level clerks—come from a socio-economic strata that is vastly different from the average people whose development becomes their charge. The gulf is only marginally less than that in the colonial times and the 'us' versus 'them' labels become inevitable. The bureaucrats, therefore, perforce have to take recourse to stereotypes to govern, and the lack of empathy and even contempt seeps in unnoticed fairly early on, creating an apathetic state machinery whose effects are evident in the speed and quality of programme implementation.

While the bureaucracy and government function-aries are the prime implementers of a policy, several other stakeholders—media, civil society (through NGO activists), legislators (MPs and MLAs), Panchayati Raj functionaries, and occasionally the judiciary (reacting to PILs)—play a key role in monitoring policy and programme implementation, and in bringing delays and corruption to light. The Mazdoor Kisan Shakti Sangathan, in its struggle against corrupt land record officials, and the Kejriwal-led NGO, Parivartan, in its campaign against corrupt fair-price shop owners, have used the mechanism of *jan sunwai*s (public hearings) for bringing officials and potential beneficiaries together, to great effect.

Management of Implementation

The earlier discussion brings out the following points:

1. Implementation is a hard challenge: major public programmes are massive enterprises operating at a gigantic scale made even more challenging in an extremely diverse country marked by poor infrastructure;

2. The key delivery machinery of project and policy implementation that comprises the entire bureaucratic hierarchy is saddled with challenges from manpower shortage, to 'fit' of capabilities, administrative challenges, inherent biases, lack of proper incentives, and monitoring; and

3. Implementation improves when policy beneficiaries get to monitor it either through political channels (legislators) or civil society organizations (NGOs).

Nevertheless, the Indian state has indeed succeeded in executing certain mind-boggling feats. The elections, held regularly in relative peace, are a global feat. The fairly safe conduct of religious fairs, including the great Kumbh Mela—world's largest human congregation—baffles the international press and academics alike, including those from the Harvard University. While general administration and policies often languish, those held in time-bound *abhiyan* or campaign mode usually do better. The polio eradication campaign is a good example. Notwithstanding the steep challenge, a reasonably good policy implementation does not appear to be an impossible challenge. Are there any basic principles that can address the implementation challenge?

This is where principles of management can come handy. While the challenges of policy implementation are indeed too varied and context-specific to be solved by a cookbook recipe for success, a few broad management principles apply to almost all of them.

1. *Setting clear, time-bound, observable, and preferably quantitative targets*: These count as indicators of

success. This is pretty much the basic for any project management. Successful project managers like E. Sreedharan, who headed the building of the Delhi Metro (as well as other large projects in his career) has used this to amazing success. The challenge with this, however, is that it works better in 'mission' mode with a specific project that gets over in a visible horizon rather than in a 'continuing' mode as in general administration. The trick here is to convert 'continuing' projects into 'mission' projects by setting periodic targets (to achieve a certain specified instance of success (like achieving 'zero backlog' by a specified date).

2. *Clarity of roles and team-building principles*: Usually policy work is about managing large teams sometimes working across vast geographies. Role clarity and specified responsibility are crucial here. This is particularly critical in actions of life and death criticality like disaster management. The standard operating procedure (SOP) of disaster management operations like those carried out by the New Delhi Municipal

Council (NDMC) clearly specify areas of responsibility and the chain of command to maximize effectiveness.

3. *Setting interim targets and adopting scientific methods of constant monitoring including an effective management information system (MIS)*: Information sharing and monitoring is one area where government projects are particularly weak. Using mobile phone apps to update inspections of physical infrastructure like roads and bridges, reduce corruption and improve response time by authorities. This is rapidly becoming standard now across states in the country.

4. *Getting the implementers to share values and to 'own' the results rather than just work to rule*: Large groups of individuals—whether in government or in private organizations—can never perform well if they only execute orders from superiors. It is extremely important to do 'team building' exercise and get to a shared vision of the project where all team members get a sense of 'ownership' of the project and work for a greater cause. This is particularly true where the need for grassroots-level innovation is high. There is

a critical need to transform the job from the 'leader's dream' to the 'dream of the team'. One of the weaknesses of the rigidly hierarchical bureaucratic practice of policy implementation is that it comes in the way of the 'team approach'. Successful ministers and senior bureaucrats succeed by investing in team building. The results framework document (RFD) approach introduced by the performance management division of the cabinet secretariat attempted to measure performance of teams rather than individual bureaucrats.

5. *Enabling, empowering, and encouraging innovations*: Almost no two instances of a policy application are identical. Instructions, however detailed, can never be complete. It is therefore imperative that the implementing team feels safe enough to experiment. The person on the ground is usually best suited to know the 'how' of delivery if the 'why' is well communicated. The bane of many of our policy implementation processes is that they are over-centralized and over specific, although they are required to be applied over a vastly diverse country or region.

6. *Proactively seeking beneficiary feedback to ensure quality*: Ultimately there is no better way to monitor projects than to go by output or outcome rather than by counting inputs. Implementing agencies are notoriously shy of beneficiary feedback, while gathering it has become amazingly simple in today's age of information technology. Railways, for instance, has become proactive in gathering feedback from travellers to figure out the quality and customer satisfaction of its services.

Implementing Administrative Turnarounds—A Case Study of Bihar 2005–12

Implementation challenges are present at all levels, from implementing a specific programme to creating a lasting improvement in general administration, law and order, and public service delivery. However, instances of perceptible improvement of state administration are perhaps a cut above the rest in terms of the scale and diversity of the problem as well as impact to the state in question as well as the country. A few episodes of such

'turnarounds' or major shifts in administrative quality have been lauded in media in the recent years—
the Chandrababu Naidu administration in Andhra
Pradesh in the pre–2004 period; the Modi administration in Gujarat, 2002–14; and the first term of the
Nitish Kumar administration in Bihar, 2005–10, to
name a few.

This section (based on Chakrabarti 2012) looks at
some of the implementation strategies of the Nitish
Kumar administration, which seem to have a few common elements with those of the other successful CMs.
The approach is to trigger thought on the implementation challenges and possible remedies rather than
act as a reference point for a fail-safe recipe of good
governance.

In 2005, Kumar was elected to run a state that was in
shambles, a virtually lawless place with decrepit roads
and a dysfunctional social infrastructure of schools and
hospitals. In six years, his administration managed to
turn it into one of the fastest-growing states in the
country. What were the strategies that Kumar adopted
to bring about this transformation?

Perhaps the central feature of the Nitish Kumar
administration was that of *empowerment with monitoring.*

The top bureaucracy as well as the middle bureaucracy was empowered significantly, with virtually a free hand to solve administrative problems, along with an assured support from the senior officials for most innovations. This was apparent in the amount of funds the officers had the jurisdiction to release. From an era when expenditures above Rs 2.5 million required cabinet approval, the regime shifted to ministers signing up to Rs 100 million on their own.

However, along with this increased empowerment and delegation came close monitoring. Never before in Bihar and rarely, if ever, elsewhere in India have senior bureaucrats and ministers reported to the CM's office as regularly as they did in the Nitish Kumar administration. There were monthly, at times fortnightly, review sessions of each department, that were attended personally by Kumar and his secretaries, with the minister and principal secretary and other secretaries reporting their progress. The bureaucrats had freedom to do what they wanted, but the results of their actions were closely monitored by Nitish himself. This was management by objectives at its best. It also helped Kumar stay on top of information in the state.

It also kept the bureaucracy under relentless pressure. Reporting to the CM every month was not a simple matter and the bureaucrats had to be completely prepared at all points in time. Slacking off was no longer an option. It is not unfair to say that Kumar flogged the bureaucracy mercilessly in delivering what they did in 2005–10.

Kumar not only pushed the bureaucracy, he also succeeded in inspiring it. The bureaucracy respects nothing more than an informed and analytical mind that is a rare find among its political masters. On that count, as well as by the personal example of his own tireless routine, Kumar extracted unhesitating respect from the bureaucracy who felt honoured to be considered part of a historic transformation. Secretaries were keen to be part of the core team, regardless of the crushing workload that such positions usually entailed.

Kumar succeeded in instilling an extremely demanding work culture within the bureaucracy. His greatest success had been in winning over the bureaucracy, motivating it and pushing it along, rather than blaming it for the shortcomings of the administration—a tempting scapegoat for many politicians. This supportive monitoring went a long way in altering the functioning of the Bihar government.

Nevertheless, the bureaucracy is not the only element in running a state. The government also functions as a cabinet. While Kumar had been respectful of his cabinet colleagues, it was not wrong to say that he ran the administration virtually from 1 Anne Marg, bypassing most of the ministers. Their authority was never undercut palpably, but just the method of monitoring with review meetings between the CM and his team and the relevant minister and secretaries created a situation where the concerned minister had to match the information and intellect of the others in the meeting or resign himself to playing a passive role. Few enterprising ministers could live up to the challenge, but most chose the comfort and prestige of their position with their secretaries reporting to the CM's secretariat and the minister serving largely as a rubber stamp. It was perhaps the only model that dragged Bihar out of the morass it had sunk to, with decisive action, but the sustainability of that model in the long run remains unclear.

While Kumar worked at energizing and pushing the bureaucracy, he solved the issue of corrupt and inept ministers by largely bypassing them in action. While they had their red beacon cars and ministerial privileges, the real action was being driven by the secretaries, monitored closely from the CM's office.

There was, however, a risk of the government losing touch with the people, because of the importance given to the bureaucracy. Kumar avoided that lacuna through his direct touch with the masses—his weekly *janta darbars* and the multiple *yatras* being important vehicles. He did not allow local politicians to be his eyes and ears any more than the bureaucrats, seeking to maintain direct contact with the populace.

Thus, Kumar succeeded in pulling off the Bihar transformation more by divorcing administration from electoral politics rather than by attempting the harder challenge of improving the level of politics to bring about the much-needed change.

A positive communication strategy also played a key role in Kumar's administration. Coming in at the nadir that Bihar had reached under the previous regime, he enjoyed some support of the media in the initial years, but then he worked hard at taking the media along. While critics would label this as nothing other than media management using the government's increasing advertisement budget, meant to advance brand Nitish, undeniably the change initiative also benefited from this. The feeling of goodwill and progress that the proactive approach to communication and media management generated had its effects on furthering public confidence in the entire change agenda. Good governance, like several other phenomena, depends on public perception and has strong self-fulfilling characteristics. A society suffused with a belief that it is being governed well will, in fact, be more likely to be receptive towards positive changes.

Things that Kumar did not do perhaps also contributed to the Bihar turnaround. He did not go about, with media in tow, to solve existing problems by attacking the establishment. It is too tempting for a politician to walk into a non-functioning school or hospital or government department on a surprise visit and haul up the chief functionary in front of the media for obvious lack of professionalism. Such actions may win the protagonist a temporary image of a change maker, but it antagonizes the establishment and the middle to lower bureaucracy without whose cooperation politicians can achieve very little. The non-functioning government offices in a badly governed system are only the symptoms; the malaise, usually, lies elsewhere. An effective approach to bring about change is the steady, uncharismatic, off-camera job of calling for files and acting on them with serious follow-up rather than flash-in-the-pan media acts of instantaneous bravado.

Political viability in Bihar's electoral and social setting demanded a shift in tactics. Kumar was extremely pragmatic when it came to elections. The same CM who would vigorously prosecute criminal-politicians would happily go along with a candidate list tainted with criminals. In Kumar's world, the legislator and the executive were unequivocally discrete. He would unhesitatingly do whatever it took to win elections and then use the mandate thus obtained to be a ruthless administrator devoted to good governance.

This approach, however, has two threats to its sustainability. The bureaucracy may not be able to sustain the high-energy routine for too long and the political class may revolt at the denial of its gravy train. Nevertheless, it worked well during the period when the state desperately needed it.

Kumar's turnaround administration in Bihar highlights sensible tactics for effectively managing the bureaucracy to achieve results in a challenging environment. However, it is but one instance of an approach that worked well at a particular place and time with no assurance of universal success. In order to understand what works and why, and for guidance to the next policy innovation or implementation best practice, the third leg of the policymaking cycle—analysis and evaluation—is of critical importance. The next chapter covers that subject.

Policy Analysis and Evaluation

Role of Evaluation in the Policy Cycle and Its Challenges

Spurred by the Supreme Court's directives to reduce the capital's pollution level, the Delhi government introduced the now famous 'odd–even' rule of vehicular rationing for the first fortnight of 2016. Like most public policy interventions, the step inconvenienced some people and brought benefits to others. At the end of the day, the questions that arose were: Did it work? Should it be repeated? Should other cities also experiment with it?

It turns out that these questions are not very easy to answer. Of course, in this particular instance, the general impression appears to be that the effect on pollution may have been marginal, but the effect on road congestion was perceptible and therefore it was a step in the right direction. Acting on this view, and after conducting a poll of sorts among Delhi residents, the government decided to repeat the experiment for another 15 days.

Policy evaluation is the least talked about and understood of the three steps of the policymaking process. Yet, without an unbiased, methodical impact assessment of past policy measures, it is virtually impossible to formulate sound policies or improve the implementation of policies. Every year, the government allocates tens of billions of taxpayers' money in various schemes—an institution of learning here, a sanitation project there, an IT-led innovation elsewhere, and so on. If these innovations are not effective, then this is tantamount to a colossal waste of public funds that, in a relatively poor country like India, can easily find more effective alternative use.

For decades, India had a slew of plans, schemes, and policies aimed at economic growth and poverty reduction. Yet, until the 1980s, India's annual growth rate remained stubbornly stuck at 3.5 per cent, a figure that had derisively been labelled as the 'Hindu rate of growth' and India's record of poverty alleviation remained uninspiring. The growth figures have risen since but there is relatively less progress on poverty alleviation. Clearly, we were not learning the lessons from our own past, and were often repeating and actually aggravating past mistakes by scaling up faulty programmes.

Policies are usually made out of public clamour and the belief—stemming from ideology or broad economic reasoning—that these are solutions to existing problems. But just as the same drug may not work equally on two individuals with the same malaise, what may have worked in a different economic context or what is generally believed to be true for ideological reasons may well prove to be ineffective or even counter-productive in another setting. While some element of a guessing game is inevitable in policymaking, not carefully analysing and learning from the past interventions is an ignorance policymakers can ill afford. Impact evaluation of policy measures is therefore an essential element of policy-making. However, it is also at least as challenging as the other two steps—formulation and implementation.

Now why is impact evaluation so difficult? Let us continue to consider the rather sharply defined intervention of the odd–even rule in Delhi. It has a definite start and end date and is imposed on a relatively small area with best-in-the-country media attention and social media coverage. The common challenges of measuring effects of policies applied to larger states and gradually phased in over time are not here. Even then, a few basic questions remain.

If we are to declare a particular policy intervention like the odd–even rule right or wrong, we have to be clear about what the policy objective is and whether the intervention is helping achieve that objective. If, as in this case, it does not worsen the primary goal of pollution reduction but actually helps reduce another major ill—traffic snarls—then it is probably a good thing to have: it is for Delhiites and the Delhi government to decide whether to have it or not for that purpose. As a solution to the pollution problem, it is probably not particularly effective.

It is therefore critical to have clarity of the purpose of evaluation: are we asking if the 'odd–even' rule is a good idea or are we asking if it is the good/best solution for pollution reduction. In either case, its effect on pollution needs to be examined. Did it reduce pollution? This turns out to be a vexing question. It is not enough to see if pollution levels were lower during its operation than before because pollution indicators themselves are time variant. Therefore, it is not clear what the contribution of the rule is to the observed change, if any, in the pollution level.

In other words, the exact question being asked here is whether the odd-even rule reduced pollution from what its levels would have otherwise been had the rule not been implemented. Now this benchmark, of course, is unobservable because the implementation of the rule itself made that option impossible. This is what is called the counterfactual. The evaluator's challenge, therefore, is to approximate this counter-factual in the best manner possible to reach the conclusion. The next section examines few such techniques.

Estimating the counterfactual to come up with the contribution of the intervention to the observed effect is, however, only the first challenge. Pretty much like choosing a drug to administer to a patient, it is also important to know what side effects the intervention had on the 'overall health' of the patient. For instance, the odd-even rule had a (quite predictable) positive side effect on the traffic congestion in the city. Just for closure, an evaluation of the odd–even rule just on its effect on pollution, carried out by researchers at the Energy Policy Institute of Chicago (EPIC), University of Chicago and Evidence for Policy Design (EPoD), Harvard, found that the initiative had reduced pollution by over 10 per cent (Greenstone et al. 2016).

Often, the entire picture cannot be obtained only by registering a few measures and indicators. It is necessary to understand the effect the change had on people's lives in a soft, qualitative, and psychological manner and equally in the way of hard, measurable effects. That is where impact evaluation begins to look more like an art than a science. The eyes of the beholder begin to play a role as opposed to cold dials and scales. And the neutrality of the evaluator immediately assumes critical importance, for the qualitative story to reflect the most unbiased if not the 'true' version of things.

Over the past few decades, impact evaluation has emerged as a field in itself. Major multilateral agencies such as the World Bank and the UN have their own independent evaluation divisions (Independent Evaluation Office and the UN Evaluations Group [UNEG] respectively) that assess the impact of their interventions effectively, acting as the umpires of success for the projects of these organizations. Aid agencies, such as the United States Agency for International Development (USAID) and UK's Department for International Development (DFID); specialized multinational consulting outfits; and think tanks, such as 3ie and the Abdul Latif Jameel Poverty Action Lab (J-PAL) of the Massachusetts Institute of Technology (MIT) carry out evaluation projects worth millions of dollars for governments around the world with reports that decide the fate of projects costing billions of dollars.

Private donors like the Bill and Melinda Gates Foundation insist on proper third-party evaluation to be carried out for each of their initiatives. Associations of evaluators like the American Evaluation Association (AEA) and UK Evaluators' Society (UKES) set standards for their members that contribute to the progressive evolution of best practices and global standards in the field just like professional bodies such as medical associations, bar associations, or associations of chartered accountants. Universities such as Carleton in Canada have started offering multidisciplinary diploma programmes in evaluation studies.

India was somewhat slow in catching up with the culture of evaluation. While assessments of programme results have occasionally been funded by the executing agency and carried out by government-funded universities for several decades, most of them do not fulfil the standards of independent impact evaluation. Governments have typically published the laudatory results and suppressed the critical ones. It was only around 2004 that the erstwhile Planning Commission made a slow start in methodically evaluating government programmes and even making it compulsory for government programmes to allocate funds towards evaluation right at the beginning of the programme. Since then quite a few programmes and schemes have been evaluated (we shall see a few of them in the third section). The Planning Commission had instituted the Independent Evaluators Office (IEO) in the final year of its existence. While the IEO has been disbanded, the NITI Aayog, the successor to the Planning Commission, has impact evaluation as one of its key objectives.

Different Methods of Evaluating Policy

As the previous section shows, evaluation is a challenging exercise requiring intricate knowledge and clever use of statistical and economic techniques. The confounding thing about policy change is that it happens neither overnight nor in a setting where other environmental elements remain static. Consequently, figuring out the impact of a specific change on the observed outcome change becomes a serious methodological challenge. In recent years, however, several standard techniques have emerged to assess the effectiveness of specific policy discussions. A broad discussion of a few of these approaches is helpful in understanding the logic of how to think about evaluating policy.

Let us begin with the most-talked-about technique for policy impact measurement, often referred to as the 'gold standard' in impact evaluation—randomized control trials (RCT). To understand the logic behind how RCT works, think for a minute about how scientists, particularly in medicine and pharmaceutical research, study the effect of drugs to see if it works or not. The standard methodology (or design of experiment in slightly technical speak) is to select a group of respondents (mice or men, depending upon the stage of drug testing) on whom the drug is likely to work (this would be a particular age–gender–race group, with or without a specific ailment). The drug is then administered to a randomly selected subset of that group called the 'treatment group'.

For human subjects, since the mind plays a big role, the remaining members, who are called the 'control group', are given a dud pill, a placebo, so that every respondent thinks he/she is getting the drug and only the experimenter knows who is in which group. After the period over which the drug is supposed to work, the effect of the drug on the two groups is compared to conclude on its effectiveness. Of course, every individual participant in the trial differs from everyone else, but since the treatment group is chosen randomly, there is likely to be no pattern that would confound this result. On the other hand, there would be various other factors present in same proportions in the two groups, so the common differences in outcome can be ascribed to the drug in question.

For ages, economists (and other social scientists) have envied the basic scientists for their access to such experimental techniques. Social scientists simply did not have the ability to test their hypothesis by turning to a group of human subjects. If they had a 'theory of change' in mind, that is, a hypothesis that intervention A (say better access to credit) produced outcome B (more successful businesses) they had no way of running an experiment to figure out empirically if the hypothesis was right. As a result they were compelled to analyse data from various situations—different countries and different periods—to argue the empirical validity or otherwise of their hypothesis.

The RCT approach seeks to change exactly that. The approach here is to administer an intervention to a *randomly* selected group of recipients from amongst a larger group of potential beneficiaries to judge the effect of the intervention exactly as the drug evaluator would do. How does it work in reality? Often, particularly in poorer countries, governments do not have the wherewithal to roll out a policy input to all potential beneficiaries, or at least in one go. For instance when the Mahatma Gandhi National Rural Employment Guarantee Scheme (MGNREGS) was rolled out, it began with a few select districts, and few blocks within those districts, and gradually spanned out, over years. Now if the RCT administrator can convince the policymaker to make his/her choice of beneficiary units (individuals, villages, or districts depending upon the intervention) randomly, rather than by aligning it to some other rule, he now has access to a 'treatment group' and a 'control group' between whom to compare the outcomes.

This, of course, is not a simple task. Firstly, policy-makers usually would have some criterion (like the poorest or most deserving by some other measure, district, block, village, or household) to base their selection of recipients of an intervention than a pure random selection just to aid a researcher. However, over time and through the tireless evangelization of this method by Abhijeet Banerjee and Esther Duflo of MIT—authors of *Poor Economics* (2011) and founders of J-PAL—the RCT approach has become accepted the world over as the most convincing research approach. Sometime because of this and sometimes because of clout and connection, J-PAL researchers (including Banerjee and Duflo themselves, along with their co-authors for the various papers) have succeeded in getting randomly allotted policy interventions (like allocation of subsidized credit among a group of eligible borrowers for instance) to carry out RCT-based studies.

Also, since major policy interventions cost the exchequer significant sums of money, the practice of using a 'pilot' to check the results before a full-scale rollout (for programmes whose effects can be noticed relatively quickly) is gaining ground. For instance, state governments, which are keen on improving immunization rates, would likely want to know if a small incentive (like a utensil) given to the mother on immunization of the child would actually improve immunization rates. Banerjee, Duflo, and their co-authors from J-PAL have done such an exercise involving 134 villages in Rajasthan, with 30 villages having monthly immunization camps, 30 having such camps with incentives, and 74 'control' villages. After an 18-month period, they came up with results which showed that the incentives did help improve immunization rates.

Of course, it is not always possible nor most suitable to carry out RCTs. Time and resource constraints (they are quite expensive) apart, they need to be planned right at the beginning of the exercise, so it is not possible to evaluate ongoing programmes using them. Also RCTs tend to have limited external validity or generalizability. For instance, in the example above, the extent to which the Rajasthan experiment would carry through in other social settings elsewhere in the country will remain an open question.

Another technique often used is the more traditional 'difference-in-difference' method. The idea here is simple: if we compare the before–after change (difference) in an outcome measure of interest for two groups and compare them (difference in difference), we get an estimate of the impact of the intervention. For example in the quick evaluation of the odd–even rule mentioned in the previous section, the approach used was to measure the difference in pollution levels (measured as concentration of certain particles in air) between Delhi (where the rule was applied) and neighbouring urban areas like Gurgaon, before and after the rule was introduced. The logic here is that if the across-region difference widened during the rule than before (which was the observed case then it must be that the rule was responsible for it, since other confounding factors like temperature and humidity changes that vary over time are likely to affect both regions.

The contentious issue with the difference-in-difference approach is the degree of similarity of the treatment and control groups. In the absence of randomization, there is always the possibility that some unobserved factor would confound the results (like keener students taking up an offered course and then doing relatively better in exams because they are more hard-working rather than because of the course itself).

There are several other statistical methods of evaluation that are used in various situations. But not all evaluation is purely quantitative. Quantitative approaches work better when the question is a pointed one (such as 'did intervention A help improve performance on objective B?'), while qualitative or 'mixed' methods are more applicable for holistic evaluations (such as 'did a particular intervention improve the quality of life of beneficiaries?').

Sometimes, of course, nothing speaks louder than data. Arguably the most damning evidence of policy failure in India comes from the *Annual Status of Education Report* (*ASER*) brought out by the education NGO, Pratham (http://www.asercentre.org/, last accessed on 15 February 2016). Started in 2005, ASER measures learning outcomes in a large sample of school-going children around the country—starting from over 330,000 children in over 8,000 schools in 2005 to more than 1,138,000 children in over 15,000 schools in 2014. It essentially tests its sample of children between ages 5 and 16 years on their level of reading and quantitative abilities, beginning at the most basic literacy levels and progressing from there.

Its findings have been startling: in 2014, for instance, it showed that school enrolment has been above 96 per cent (for the sixth year in a row) and attendance above 70 per cent, though with very significant interstate variation. But about half of the standard V students and about a quarter of standard VIII students cannot read a simple standard II text! Worse, these rates have shown no sign of improvement in the past 6 years. Children going to private schools do better than those from government schools but even in that case, more than a quarter of standard V students cannot read standard II text! About 40 per cent of students in standards II and III cannot recognize numbers up to 100!

Nobody asked Pratham to invest this energy and effort into doing an evaluation of the children's learning levels, essentially a task that the public authorities should have been doing. But the *ASER* has now established itself as the nation's trusted benchmark in assessing the degree of effectiveness (or lack thereof) in primary education. This is not by using any complicated evaluation methodology but by simply providing stark data that has been painstakingly and accurately collected—data against which no arguments or excuses can hold water. State governments are pushed to at least accept this reality and hopefully contemplate remedial policy action. Critically important here is the independence of the agency—the ASER centre of Pratham in this case—in undertaking the survey.

Not all policy analysis has to be highly statistical, however. Nor are quantitative approaches capable of capturing the human effects of policy changes. 'All that counts, cannot be counted' as Einstein is believed to have said. Interviews from carefully sampled stakeholders or beneficiaries, and focused group discussions often supplement or can even substitute quantitative approaches.

Findings from Certain Significant Evaluation Studies about India

Notwithstanding India's somewhat delayed entry into the world of policy evaluation, the number of evaluative works on Indian policy intervention—some commissioned to independent third parties by government agencies like the erstwhile Planning Commission or by multilateral donor bodies like the World

Bank or DFID and some by academic researchers themselves—have quickly piled up. After all, one thing that India has continued to enjoy right since its independence is the attention of top development economists including, but certainly going far beyond, some of the best ones who happen to hail from India itself. Some of the findings of these evaluation studies are already being used in improving policy delivery design.

Take, for instance, the work done by University of California, San Diego economist Karthik Muralidharan and his co-authors in evaluating the delivery of MGNREGS and Social Security Pension (SSP) payments using biometric Aadhaar cards in Andhra Pradesh (around 2010–12) (Muralidharan, Niehaus, and Sukhtankar n.d.). Working with the Government of Andhra Pradesh, they created a large-scale experiment that randomized the rollout of smartcards over 158 sub-districts and 19 million people. Their finding: the new system delivered a faster, more predictable, and less corrupt NREGS payments process without adversely affecting programme access. It significantly reduced 'leakages' and the beneficiaries also overwhelmingly preferred the new system for both programmes. The effect of this study on policymaking: adoption of a three-step new method of fund distribution in MGNREGS directly from the central government to the panchayats as opposed to the old nine-step system (*Economic Survey* 2016).

Now was there a need to run a full-blown RCT experiment to make the point? Is it not obvious that smartcards would reduce leakage and make payments more efficient? Well, not quite. Contrary to the overwhelming preference for smartcards among beneficiaries (92 per cent in the experiment), the feedback from field functionaries that reached the state officials stressed the problems of using smartcards in such a vocal manner that the state government almost came close to scrapping the Aadhaar payment model in 2013. This points to the power of vested interests in distorting perceptions.

In fact, the authors speculate that the intervention could continue because of a Supreme Court ruling which said that the government could not make the use of smartcards mandatory in delivering the benefits. Thus, the vested interest of parasitical intermediaries, though reduced, was not completely eliminated, which allowed for the continuation of the programme. In the absence of this scientific survey, the overwhelming but diffuse positive voice would have been drowned by the few vocal ones, whose source of corrupt income was threatened by the new mechanism.

A host of other policies have been studied to establish the connection between the intervention and its effects as well as the role of other factors that affected the outcome. These include the effect of the famous 'bicycle for schoolgirls' intervention of the Bihar CM Nitish Kumar wherein girl students reaching standard IX were given money to purchase a bicycle to go to a school that was likely to be a little distant from their village(s). The premise was that travelling the distance safely was the biggest challenge contributing to girls dropping out of school at that level. Did it work?

The answer could never be clear unless a formal evaluation was carried out. Theories and stereotypes abounded on both sides. The anecdotes of girls' parents stopping them from going to school fearing for their safety as they reached puberty would be matched by the infamous stereotype of the alcoholic father drinking away the money given for purchasing the daughter's bicycle. Ultimately only a scientific inquiry into the question could settle the debate. The challenge here was also that it could not be evaluated using the RCT approach since the scheme did not begin in a randomized manner.

However, the evaluation that was carried out used data from a large representative household survey and it cleverly employed a 'triple difference approach' (using boys as well as data of the neighbouring state of Jharkhand as comparison groups). It found that being in a group which was exposed to the bicycle programme increased girls' age-appropriate enrolment in secondary school by 30 per cent and also reduced the gender gap in the age–appropriate secondary school enrolment by 40 per cent. Apart from establishing the effectiveness of the programme it also found that the bicycle programme was much more cost effective at increasing girls' enrolment than comparable conditional cash transfer programmes in South Asia, indicating other benefits like improved safety from girls cycling to school in groups, and changes in patriarchal social norms that proscribed female mobility outside the village, which inhibited female secondary school participation.

These are, of course, but only two examples of evaluations of policy measures that have had important implications for policymaking and have actually completed the loop to find their way into policy improvements. Most of the time policymakers do not have the benefit of 'evidence-based policymaking', simply because evaluations take time and are sometimes context dependent. What do they base their decisions on then? John Maynard Keynes (1936) had famously observed that 'even the most practical man of affairs is usually in the thrall of the ideas of some long-dead economist'.

This problem, 'ossified ideas' as the former chief economic advisor to the Government of India and current chief economist of the World Bank, Kaushik Basu (2015) calls it, continues to be a major challenge among policymakers in India. There is nothing wrong with approaching an issue with a certain 'theory of change' in mind, but being inflexible about such a model is where the trouble begins. Being dogmatic about paradigms is usually a problem in a policymaker, for unlike the laws of physics, the relationships of social science are rarely universal. The quest for evidence, for checking every policy step and looking for areas of improvements must, therefore, be a key step in effective policymaking.

Convincing with Evidence: Policy Advocacy

Evaluation studies of policy interventions are now being increasingly built into the interventions themselves. However, trying out new policy steps is not something that the government is very good at doing by itself. The bureaucracy is not incentivized to experiment—if an innovative initiative works out, it is quite likely that the kudos will go to the successor of the innovator, given the few years it may take for the initiative to fructify, while any problems or negative early signs is likely to besmirch the innovator's reputation and career prospects. As a result the very first question that one hears when proposing a new policy idea is one of precedence: 'Has this been done somewhere in the government before?' The average politician or bureaucrat is also stuck too deeply in the rut of daily work to find the time to look around for policy experiments being tried out elsewhere in the world or other states in India itself. There comes the relevance of policy advocacy groups.

The advocacy groups have varied stances and can torpedo the rare policy innovations coming from government as well. For example, in 2011, Kaushik Basu, the then chief economic adviser to the Government of India, had suggested that, to encourage reporting, in cases where bribes had to be given to officials to get legitimate work done, the bribe giver be exempted from punishment. This idea was opposed by many prominent activists on the grounds that it would reduce the stigma of corruption, that mechanisms for reporting were already in place, etc. The negative reaction, based on presumptions rather than data, drowned the suggestion.

Policy advocacy groups range from corporates that can benefit from the government adopting a particular policy to non-profit special interest groups working towards causes ranging from environmental protection to human rights to pure policy research groups like the London School of Economics based International Growth Centre (IGC). These groups routinely interact with ministers and bureaucrats to suggest new policy ideas to them. Take for instance the Bill and Melinda Gates Foundation's work in the health sector in India as well as other developing countries. They focus on public health issues such as eradication of tuberculosis, malaria, and AIDS.

Governments are increasingly becoming receptive to the ideas from these advocacy groups particularly when they come with funding. This is because increasingly the government finds itself incapable of implementing grassroots-level changes, say in health and education. Over time, governments in India—at the centre as well as states—have come around to accept the superiority of the private sector in management of large initiatives, and is open, even keen, to forge partnerships with private organizations, particularly if the private party's initiatives are self-funded.

The biggest weapon of the policy advocacy groups in selling their ideas to the government is, of course, evidence. As a result, the policy advocacy bodies need to carry out their own independent evaluation studies to build a case for pushing their agendas within the government.

Consider the San-Francisco-based, global climate advocacy group founded by George Soros, Climate

Policy Initiative's operations in India (http://climate-policyinitiative.org/india/). Its advocacy agenda centres around pushing renewable sources of energy in India. It actively pursues this agenda through research that focuses on the roadblocks in the adoption of renewable energy (for instance, high cost of finance) and suggests ways around them by analysing international practices. It also highlights and discusses examples of successful renewable policy initiatives, like the 100 Megawatt (MW) Rajasthan Sun Technique Concentrated Solar Power (CSP) Plant in Rajasthan which it pitches to policymakers.

Focused Indian advocacy groups like the Centre for Civil Society (CCS) (http://www.ccs.in) or the Centre for Competition, Investment and Economic Regulation of the Consumer Unity and Trust Society (CUTS-CCIER) (http://www.cuts-ccier.org/) carry out research to put together evidence that they use in convincing policymakers to take steps towards their policy agenda.

The IGC is perhaps the biggest international-development-focused research group looking at development issues in virtually all developing countries around the world. Funded by the UK's DFID, it

is a loose network of leading development economics researchers from around the world, but primarily
the UK and the US. It has two centres in India—the
IGC India based in New Delhi (http://www.theigc.
org/country/india-central/) and IGC Bihar based
in Patna (http://www.theigc.org/country/india-
bihar/)—working with partner institutions, the Indian
Statistical Institute and Asian Development Research
Institute (ADRI), respectively. While it does not have
a specific policy agenda to advocate it focuses its
research efforts in the following areas: firm produc-
tivity growth, urbanization, infrastructure, energy, and
state effectiveness (including macroeconomics, finance,
and human development). In a few short years, the
IGC has produced an extremely impressive body of
research that ranges from evaluation of specific programmes to broad findings that can affect national
policy directions—from investigation discrimination
in school uniform and scholarship schemes in Bihar
to the effect of female politicians in economic growth
across the country.

A key element of the IGC's research is also advocacy,
but of a somewhat different kind than, say what
Climate Policy Initiative (CPI) would be undertaking.

IGC would work hard towards exposing policymakers to its research findings—through periodic workshops and conferences bringing together academics and policymakers; by communicating its research in easily intelligible and forceful manner to policymakers; and/or by summarizing its findings in its non-technical outlet, Ideas for India (www.ideasforindia.in). It is the respectability and global stature of its researchers as well as the convincing ability of its output that makes its research a potential thought-changer for the government and works as a conduit for connecting cutting-edge research and evidence to flow into policymaking.

Companies—predominantly MNCs but also increasingly Indian companies—also undertake research and analysis with a view to convince policymakers towards undertaking policy measures that align with their corporate interests. Here, of course, given the presence of clear conflict of interest, the research becomes acceptable only if it is actually undertaken by a third party of immaculate reputation. More than individual companies, the industry associations and chambers of commerce—CII and FICCI or ASSOCHAM in India—regularly undertake studies and publish reports that put together data and ideas with recommendations for the government. Given that the industry associations invest a significant effort in connecting with the government and are seen as the voice of industry, they are, in fact, a major source of policy input for the minister and bureaucrat contemplating policy formulation and framing an implementation mechanism that affects these stakeholders.

★ ★ ★

The formulation–implementation–analysis cycle is a continuous spiral that keeps policymaking abreast with never-ending changes in the real world. The difference between great policymaking and playing the game of catching up lies in the ability of the policy system to analyse and anticipate environmental changes and frame policies in a manner that will be effective in the reality of tomorrow rather than in the context of yesterday. Just as a visionary leader is better attuned with the future than a mere pragmatist, effective policymaking mechanism must have within it the flexibility to keep adjusting to a changing environment.

The conclusion about species often attributed to Darwin—the ones that survive are neither necessarily the strongest nor most intelligent but the most adaptable—is also true of good policies. Making and implementing policies for a rapidly changing world is almost like cooking a delicacy or treating a patient—one regularly needs to check the taste and the vital signs, respectively, and to accordingly adjust the ingredients and dosage.

The next chapter looks at how major forces that are changing the ground realities are also throwing new challenges for policymaking and what policymaking needs to do to stay abreast of these changes and use them to its advantage.

5

Strengthening Policymaking in India

In 2011, the richest part of India, Chandigarh, enjoyed a per capita income similar to St. Vincent and the Grenadines, a comfortably middle-income country, while the poorest part, Bihar, with less than a quarter of Chandigarh's per capita income, resembled Eritrea, one of the world's poorest nations. There is not one India but many 'Indias' with vastly differing income levels, varying needs, and diverse aspirations and expectations from policymakers.

All these 'Indias' are changing fast. A quarter century of liberalization has made India one of the fastest-growing large countries in the world. This has produced pockets of significant wealth: in 2010, India boasted as many billionaires as Germany that has four times India's per capita income. A sizeable middle class with purchasing power and increasing political voice has emerged. Call centres have created pockets of youth prosperity and women empowerment. The skylines of the metropolitan areas are fast changing with multi-million rupees luxury apartment buildings and glitzy malls flashing prosperity and raising aspirations. Rapid urbanization is expected to double India's share of urban population by 2030.

Economic heft and growth have also added to India's international clout with membership of clubs like the G-20. Yet economic challenges are far from over. During 2005–12 India's GDP grew by a respectable 54 per cent, but its number of jobs grew only by 3 per cent. Maoist groups operate in as many as a third of the country's districts.

A lot of this change is, of course, for the good. A study of Dalit households in Uttar Pradesh's Azamgarh and Bulandshahar districts (Prasad et al. 2010) captures the extent of transformation in their lives between 1990 and 2007. In 1990, about 3 per cent of the Dalits used toothpaste, while less than 1 per cent used shampoo. By 2007, the combined figure for both toothpaste and shampoo consumption had jumped to 65 per cent. Use of packaged salt had skyrocketed from 1 per cent to 70 per cent. Ownership of TV had soared from below 1 per cent to 34 per cent, pucca houses from 40 per cent to 77 per cent. Their relationship with non-Dalits had gone through a sea-change—at most weddings the Dalits were no longer required to sit separately, non-Dalit mid-wives had started attending Dalit mothers, and girl schooling climbed. Change has been universal in India, including in affluent urban pockets.

India has also become more vulnerable to the shifts of global economic tectonics today. The share of international trade grew from 14 per cent of GDP in 1991 to 42 per cent in 2013. In 2008, global shocks arising from the financial collapse in the West, crashed its exchange rates and stock markets, threatened its fiscal balance, and soured its export prospects. Indian manufacturers struggle to compete with a flood of cheap Chinese goods in the market while a growing section of the upper middle class is getting plugged into global fashion trends.

Finally, technology is accelerating the change manifold. India has one of the world's highest mobile penetration rates, election pledges now include free Wi-Fi connectivity, and social media is helping mobilize flash mobs as during the Nirbhaya protests and the Lokpal movement.

The policymakers of today and tomorrow have to grapple with this diversity, rapid change, global shocks, and continuously evolving technology to do their job well. They need to get used to a very different pace of change and nature of demands from the public. Their mindset, stereotypes, and, most importantly, working style need to change, for the India of their textbooks is fast disappearing.

The idea and practice of public policy have been undergoing major changes as well. Back in 1992, the Eighth Five Year Plan articulated the need to re-examine and re-orient the role of the government emphasizing two basic objectives: (a) allowing entry of private sector in areas hitherto the domain of the public sector; and (b) increasing the scope for citizens to participate in policy planning through voluntary agencies, panchayats, and cooperatives. This aligned well with the concept of 'good governance', a term probably first used by the World Bank in 1989, that has quickly gained currency worldwide.

Over time the phrase has come to mean more open, transparent, and participative systems of governance with 'development of governing styles in which boundaries between and within public and private sectors have become blurred' (Stoker 1998: 17). The monopoly of political institutions over governance has steadily reduced around the world, the activities that were earlier indisputably in their domain now increasingly seen as more common, generic, societal issues that can be best resolved by cooperation between multiple actors—both state and non-state.

Governance is increasingly seen as 'concerned with the network of relationships of three actors—state, market and civil society' (Mathur 2013). The Tenth Five Year Plan (2002–7) defined the state's role as creating a 'conducive political, legal and economic environment for building individual capabilities and encouraging private initiative. The market is expected to create opportunities for people. Civil society facilitates the mobilisation of public opinion and peoples' participation in economic, social and political activities.'

Notwithstanding the timely proclamation, the changeover to this model of governance from the traditional, top-down command system requires several shifts. The key roadblocks to good governance include lack of public participation in policymaking, poor public service delivery, lack of well-trained personnel, information gap due to paucity of data, and absence of systematic research due to little academia–government connect, narrow compartmentalization of activities in departments, and centralized system of policymaking with little input from the states.

The next section looks at some of these issues more closely. The third section discusses a few broad challenges specific to India that policymakers need to be particularly conscious of.

From Government to Governance— Overcoming Challenges to Open, Participative Policymaking

Creating the Right Environment for Collaboration

Revisiting the Government–Public Contract

While there has been a paradigm shift in Indian society, elements of the political and bureaucratic class have generally lagged behind the change. This has led to what Yogendra Yadav (2008) calls the paradox of political representation—the broadening of the base of political representatives has not led to a corresponding qualitative change in the nature of representation in terms of performance of the representative and the issues and concerns that get reflected in the policy agenda.

The relationship between the government and the public can take several forms: ruler–subject, agent–principal to partners in progress. During the first few decades since Independence, India witnessed a clear shift from the first stage of the colonial legacy to the second stage. The public had come to trust periodic elections to appoint a government to serve their needs, and carry their voice.

In the last couple of decades a decline in the legitimacy of the elected office-holders in the public eye has accompanied a perceptible impatience and eagerness of a section of the populace (the middle-class) to engage in governance. The desire to exercise citizenship rights and participate in policy matters well beyond passive voting in elections is now evident—the Lokpal agitation being perhaps the biggest example of that. Social movements such as the right to information movement, anti–child-labour movement, and the right to food movement challenged the discourses of the state by mobilizing people at the grassroots, with civil society organizations enjoying far greater public faith than elected representatives.

In the past, mass agitations were mostly about religious nationalism or caste identity, or demand for preferential treatment. Many recent protests have had a different character: asking the government to perform its basic duties of governance and service delivery. A rising middle class (by some estimates 250 million strong) has increasingly become cynical of the electoral process and yet wants its voice heard in policymaking.

Need to Broad-base Participation in Policymaking

To be fair, in recent years the government has also become more open to public opinion, even if only reluctantly. Putting in place a process for pre-legislative scrutiny of bills is an example. Following consultations with NGOs, activists, and certain scientists who were not convinced about the safety of genetically modified crops, the then environment minister, Jairam Ramesh, put a moratorium on the commercial testing of Bt brinjal in 2010. In fact, in some ways, the creation and operation of the unelected National Advisory Council during the UPA was an extremely unusual step in fostering civil society participation in policymaking.

While business–politics entente is increasingly common in India, lobbying by corporate and interest groups remains a grey area. Often mistaken with bribing, lobbying should be seen as a legitimate activity in a representative democracy since it provides governments with valuable policy-related information and expertise. Regulations should serve as a tool to enhance transparency rather than restricting access to policymakers.

Laws, such as the Right to Information Act, 2005, that allows citizens to request for information related to public entities, act as powerful tools of accountability and transparency. However, a number of attempts have been made by the government to curtail the scope of the act or make it less effective through lack of engaged personnel.

In the marketplace of ideas, different citizens groups now work to influence the policymaking process through a variety of ways but the government remains the final arbiter.

Working towards Better Policy Formulation

Improving the Quality of Laws

The quality of laws enacted in India leave a lot to be desired. Certain proxies such as the number of enacted laws struck down by the Supreme Court or the high courts on grounds of constitutional invalidity and the percentage of laws amended subsequently by Parliament within 3–5 years can act as indicators of the quality of a law. For example, the Competition Act of 2002 was challenged in court for violating the principle of separation of powers. It had to be amended in 2007 before the law could be operationalized.

At times, the government resorts to the power of ordinances to bypass Parliament if they are unsure of getting the numbers to enact it. Provided as a tool for exceptional cases in between Parliamentary sessions, ordinances have been used since 1954 to temporarily bypass the legislature. Many democracies including the UK, the US, Australia, and Canada do not provide ordinance powers to the executive, providing instead for emergency session of the legislature.

Poor quality of drafting is a common problem with Indian laws, something that even Hamid Ansari, the vice president, has chided the government for in the Rajya Sabha itself (*Economic Times* 2015). For instance, the 2013 land acquisition law made an obvious language error in section 113 (Removing Difficulties). This section is provided to make minor changes without changing the intent or impact of the act when faced with implementation difficulties. However, the error here made changes virtually impossible for this act.

Most bills do not have a detailed analysis of their financial implications on the exchequer. The financial memorandum of a bill only provides a lump sum figure without any details. It also does not take into account the additional implementation cost to the exchequer at the state level even though the bill may mandate that infrastructure be set up at the state level. Furthermore, there is no analysis of the manpower that would be required to implement the law. Many authorities set up by a law require implementation at the district level and the work is delegated to the district magistrate without taking into account the additional burden put on that office. Implementation is the inevitable victim.

What lessons can we learn from other countries? In the US, the Plain Writing Act, 2010, mandates drafting in an intelligible manner. The Office of the

Parliamentary Counsel of the UK provides drafting guidance to lawmakers. Additionally, many countries require periodic review of laws.

Adding to Legislative Capability

Parliament is responsible for enacting laws, scrutinizing and passing the budget, and overseeing the executive. However, individual MPs in India have little incentive to examine bills and form their own opinions because the anti-defection law makes it mandatory to vote along party lines if a whip is issued. Also, MPs need extensive and high-quality research support to learn about the various bills they need to debate upon. But they do not have research staff to help them in the matter.

Over the years, the time spent discussing the budget (general discussion as well as discussion on reports of DRSCs on Demands for Grants) has reduced from an average of 123 hours in the 1950s to 41 hours between 1994 and 2014. In 2013, all Demands for Grants, amounting to Rs 16,600 billion, were voted and passed without any discussion in the house. In 2014–15, 94 per cent of the Demands for Grants were nixed. (Shankar 2014).

Given the importance of the oversight function of Parliament in ensuring better policies, it is useful to find ways to strengthen the process. Most developed countries provide high-quality office staff and infrastructure to their legislators. Typically, in the US, a legislator is provided office space next to Congress, and a staff of about 18 to 60 persons with a limit of over Rs 40 million per year. The strength of the staff varies, depending on whether the legislator is a member of the House of Representatives or the Senate. In the UK, the cost of office space and salary of staff members are reimbursed to MPs to the tune of Rs 8.6 million per year. The US has the well-staffed Congressional Research Service (CRS) to provide policy and legal analysis to committees and legislators. The CRS experts assist at every stage of the legislative process—from the early considerations that precede drafting of bills, through committee hearings and floor debate, to the oversight of enacted laws and various agency activities. Similarly, the UK, Australia, and New Zealand have the office of Parliamentary Research Service for their legislators.

Many countries have a specialized body dedicated to conducting essential budget-related and financial research for Parliament, such as the Congressional Budget Office of the US, Office for Budget Responsibility of the UK), and the Parliamentary Budget Office of Australia, set up through acts of the legislature. These are non-partisan research bodies that provide legislators with neutral and high-quality analysis of fiscal matters that is independent of the executive. Typically, they focus on analysing the full budget cycle, the broad fiscal challenges facing the government, and the financial implications of legislative proposals.

Towards More Effective Implementation

Improving Public Service Delivery

By far the largest issue facing government agencies today is their inability to deliver public services in a transparent, time-bound manner that upholds the rule of law which cannot be subverted by cronyism and nepotism. Achieving this objective requires a focus on designing agencies efficiently, giving them clear functions, and creating a fine balance between independence and accountability.

However, India's administrative machinery has changed very slowly from the British times. A number of committees were set up to restructure the administrative agencies including the two Administrative Reforms Commissions (ARCs) in the 1960s and 2000s. The second ARC, set up in 2004 under Veerappa Moily, gave a series of reports on a range of subjects—RTI, labour management, crisis management, ethics and fiscal management, to name a few. There is little clarity on the status of implementation of most of the key suggestions. The remarkable overlap between suggestions of the first ARC (1966) and the second, four decades apart, point to a singular failure in adopting most of the much-needed reforms.

Right to Public Services: This is not to say the government has not attempted any reforms. In the period 2005–15, it adopted a two-pronged approach to address the problem of public service delivery. Based on the model law floated by the central government, many state governments such as Madhya Pradesh, Bihar, Karnataka, and Jharkhand enacted the right to public services laws to guarantee time-bound delivery of public services for citizens. These laws cover a wide range of basic services—like caste certificates and other paperwork—and make it mandatory for the bureaucracy to deliver on applications within specified time limits.

Use of Information Technology: E-governance has increasingly become the tool for facilitating these services. For example, the Karnataka government's highly regarded SAKALA Services Act created an e-portal (in addition to registers) to capture information about requests and disposals to ensure timely delivery of services. The biggest game-changer here is the Aadhaar system introduced in the UPA II regime (see chapters 3 and 4) that seeks to serve as the platform for direct, digital delivery of various subsidies.

Adopting the PPP Model of Service Delivery: The relative inability of government to manage large organizations providing service in a leakage-free manner has now come to be widely accepted. A remedy has been the adoption of the Public Private Partnership (PPP) model—like in highly visible infrastructure projects like roadways and prominent airports—in delivery of services like water supply and electricity in several cities.

However, the PPP models bring their own challenges. Take for instance the PPP approach to provide e-governance through common service centres (CSCs). Several private sector organizations had bid for mobilizing village-level entrepreneurs to build and operate CSCs which would become nodes for government's provision of e-services. One such organization was SREI Infrastructure Ltd's 'Sahaj e-Village' initiative that won the contract to set up over 28,000 CSCs in six states. After Sahaj had put up over 21,000 kiosks in a 12-month frame, delays by state governments in identifying services that would be delivered online to be accessed through the CSCs put the financial viability of these kiosks and the livelihood of the entrepreneurs and the private partner (Sahaj) at risk. Even PPP requires delivering on commitments.

Increasing Accountability: There are also scattered examples of the government's attempts to increase accountability and curb corruption. In 2005–6, for example, the ministries started outcome budgeting, a progress report on how the ministries and departments have implemented the budgetary outlays. Performance monitoring of central ministries was introduced in 2009 through the concept of Government Performance

Management. Lokayuktas were established in a number of states to address citizen's grievances about corruption. However, there is no clear evidence of how successful these measures have been in increasing accountability and curbing corruption.

Need for Capacity Building in Administration

As we pointed out in Chapter 3, a key component in re-designing government agencies to ensure better delivery of services is to staff them with adequate and competent personnel to discharge their functions efficiently. Apart from personnel deficit, the issue of quality in the sense of competence and domain expertise are becoming increasingly important here. With rising complexity in virtually every area of governance, there is need for people with domain expertise rather than generalist administrators.

The 10th report of the second ARC (Second Administrative Reforms Commission 2008) has suggested reforms in the civil services ranging from recruitment and training to promotions and performance evaluations. It has also suggested allowing lateral entry to induct the best talent in the system. Nandan

Nilekani, one of the founders of the information technology (IT) giant, Infosys, as Chairman (cabinet rank) of the Unique Identification Authority of India (UIDAI) drove the design and implementation of the game-changing Aadhaar system. In 2009, Prajapati Trivedi, an expert in government performance management, was brought in from the World Bank in the rank of a Secretary at the Cabinet Secretariat to create and implement the Results-Framework-Document (RFD) method of Performance Evaluation. The Delhi Dialogue Commission, a think tank of the Aam Aadmi Party (AAP) advertised for a number of consultants in different areas, including public policy. The government of Bihar set up the Bihar Vikas Mission to drive effective planning and execution of key government programmes. It plans to recruit a number of professionals to manage the work.

These cases, however, are still exceptions to the general rule of keeping government initiatives a privy of generalist career civil servants. Engaging with the budding policy research sector in the country would be another step in addressing the lack of trained personnel. Initiatives such as PRS Legislative Research, Swaniti, and Centre for Legislative Research and Advocacy provide internship and fellowship opportunities with MPs, offering them research support.

Enabling Better Policy Analysis

Better Coordination and Access to Information

Having access to necessary information is critical to the quality of policymaking. Information asymmetries between levels of government and between government and academia/think tanks is a serious problem in India since ministries and even departments within ministries work in silos. The first ARC had suggested that an 'office of planning and policy' be created in each ministry for the purpose of overall planning and formulation of policy but it was never implemented.

Good quality data is a critical input for any policymaking. However, India has yet to travel a distance before becoming an information-driven economy. The premier resource for public data about India, https://data.gov.in, is a good attempt by the National Informatics Centre (NIC) to curate and disseminate data from a wide range of government departments. Nevertheless, however slick the interface, the quality and reliability of the underlying information relies on the inputs of the individual ministries and government departments.

This is where there are serious issues—poor quality data, outdated resources and mismatch of numbers in different sources. Consider this. While skill development is a key challenge for the country and admitted as one for the last seven years, there is no reliable estimate sector-wise, state-level skill gap. There is no data on unit labour costs, capacity utilization of capital which are essential to frame labour and manufacturing policies. Ministry of Statistics and Programme Implementation's National Sample Survey Office (NSSO) collects periodic data on poverty levels, consumption patterns, and employment but there are inconsistencies with data collected by the Central Statistical Organization (CSO). Methodology is also an issue: CSO compiles data on service sector output but the methodology does not correspond to international best practices which make global comparisons impossible.

India could learn some lessons from other countries as to how to bridge the information gap. For example, member countries of the Organisation for Economic Co-operation and Development (OECD), such as

Australia, Sweden, Finland, Ireland, Norway, and the UK, have used advisory and governing boards to coordinate between ministries and agencies. These bodies bridge the information gap between busy political authorities and the public sector managers leading the agencies. In South Africa, the Constitution mandates that institutions to promote and facilitate intergovernmental relations are established by law.

Data collection is highly developed in the US and the OECD countries. For example, in the US, over 70 federal agencies collect data on a variety of topics. These include Bureau of the Census, Bureau of Economic Analysis, Bureau of Justice Statistics, Bureau of Labor Statistics, Library of Congress, and FedStats. The Billion Prices Project at MIT scours the Internet on a real-time basis for data from online retailers, and compiles and cleans it to extract daily measures of inflation as well as cross-country real exchange rates.

New Challenges for India's Policymakers

Regulating the Private Sector

India's economic liberalization in the 1990s opened the door for the private sector to operate in areas which were earlier government monopolies. With that came the need to shift the governance paradigm from providing to regulating, a process that is still in progress. As repeated headline-grabbing scams in the last decade over allocation of natural resources—from airwave spectrum (the 2G scam) to coal linkage—have demonstrated, the necessary processes are still in the making. Auctions are the most preferred allocation process around the world and in both cases, the Supreme Court stated that auction was the preferable way to allocate natural resources, but could not be held to be a constitutional requirement. Experts have also pointed out that revenue maximization may not be the only policy objective, in which case other options such as first-come–first-serve could be used. Allocative efficiency of auctions also depends a lot on the mechanism design—the rules of the auction.

India has also created several 'independent' sector regulators in a variety of sectors such as electricity, telecommunications, insurance, securities market, and oil and gas. This is also an increasingly common international approach to ensure fairness.

But regulators need to be regulated as well. Regulatory bodies need to be staffed with a mix of technical, administrative, and legal experts. Most of these bodies in India have served to provide sinecures to favoured civil servants, instead of getting experts of repute.

Furthermore, regulators suffer from a certain 'democratic deficit' as owing to insufficient parliamentary oversight of regulators. Legislators need to find time to understand and monitor regulators. For instance in the 15th Lok Sabha, of the 11,216 discussions held, only 9 discussions pertained to an independent regulator (these included discussions on legislation introduced in Parliament to amend statutes for establishing regulators). In the 16th Lok Sabha, until the winter session of 2015, out of 3,889 discussions, only 2 were related to independent regulators.

Harnessing India's Demographic Dividend and Averting the Demographic Disaster

India has the youngest population in the world and is on its way to overtake China as home to the world's largest workforce by 2030. With a tiny formal sector employing less than 15 per cent of the workforce and an agricultural sector mired with excess labour, this 'demographic dividend' poses arguably the biggest policy challenge for the country—finding jobs for all the new entrants to the workforce.

Poor education and skilling make most of India's youth unemployable. According to the National Association of Software and Service Companies (NASSCOM), only 25 per cent engineering graduates are directly employable in the IT industry. Also, the Aspiring Minds' 2015 *National Employability Report for Engineering Graduates* shows that only 18 per cent of the graduates are employable for the software services sector, 3 per cent in IT product sector, and about 40 per cent in business process outsourcing (BPO) organizations. Only about 10 per cent of India's Master of Business Administration (MBA) graduates are employable.

On the skilling side, while countries like US, China, Australia, and South Korea boast of 60 per cent plus of their working age population 'skilled' through some formal training programme, India's skill development figures are below 5 per cent of the population.

This problem is exacerbated by the lack of jobs in the market. It is estimated that during the five-year period from 2004–5 to 2009–10, only 2.7 million net additional jobs were created in the country. Between 2005 and 2012, the cumulative formal sector job growth was 3 per cent as opposed to a 54 per cent cumulative GDP growth. With a regulatory environment notoriously unfriendly to new entrepreneurs— India consistently features in the lowest third of the world in terms of the 'Ease of Doing Business' index, as an indicator—new jobs are simply not keeping up with the rising workforce.

The governments of the day have woken up to the challenge of skill development but design and implementation issues dog the policy initiatives in this area. Human capability, unlike physical infrastructure, cannot be created overnight, and the clock is ticking for the country.

This is, of course, much more than a purely economic issue for the country. The world around, the size of the 'not in employment, education, or training' (NEET) population is increasingly being recognized as the core driver of socio-political unrest from riots to global problems like the Islamic State of Iraq and Syria (ISIS). Closer home, the Maoist insurgency as well problems in the North-East and Kashmir may well have their solution in finding jobs for the youth.

The Jat rampage of early 2016 is also believed to be primarily a result of this problem.

Globalization and Its Political Fallout

Globalization is here to stay. This implies, foremost, mobility of capital across borders, while labour remains far more stuck to its country of origin. Many argue China's growth story was built on the country's ability to attract FDI by creating the environment for cheap manufacturing that could then exploit its virtually unending labour supply. This is much harder to do in democratic India and it is unclear whether the China model is desirable for Indians in all its aspects. However, India does need significant capital investment to create enterprises to generate growth and jobs and global investors are a key source. Even Indian investors now have a choice to export their capital if the country's policies are not favourable. This, effectively, imposes what author and commentator Tom Friedman calls the 'golden straitjacket'—a set of rules to participate in the global economy—irrespective of the domestic demands. This is a tightrope that policymakers have to walk carefully, but exit is not an option.

Globalization has also brought in greater uncertainty and volatility in the country's economy. Today, the Indian economy is increasingly prone to the vagaries of sub-prime lenders of the US in the 'tapering' by the Federal Reserve. The policymakers' degrees of freedom are being progressively curtailed.

Globalization encourages private enterprise and free competition on a global scale and this has accelerated technological innovations and entrepreneurial talents. On the negative side, many people in less developed countries have been left without safety nets. Markets are good at creating wealth but are not designed to take care of other social needs. But globalization has also helped create horizontal networks among NGOs and other institutions of accountability which has helped bring pressure on often unresponsive governments of developing nations.

For India, it has meant increased mobility of capital, goods, data, and ideas. But it has also led to reduction in subsidies and farm incomes where majority of the population is still employed. It has also meant pressure on the government to not just open up the market but also submit to environmental and social conditions. For instance, the issue of child labour got international attention when Kailash Satyarthi, Nobel laureate and child activist, advocated for boycotting trade with industries which used child labour (carpet, fireworks, etc.) and gave teeth to the advocacy.

Elsewhere, the increased availability of a range of consumer goods owing to globalization led to a mini retail-revolution in the country complete with shopping malls, bars, and fashion revolution. Mobile phones and social media made at least a section of Indian society completely connected with world opinion. Internet has revolutionized the way people access information and communicate with each other. India's monetary policy is affected by the vagaries of the global financial system. When the controversy at Jawaharlal Nehru University (JNU), New Delhi, erupted in February 2016, the University of Minnesota, among other major global institutions, expressed solidarity with the university.

Managing the global pressures while serving the interest of the Indian citizens will continue to be a key challenge for the Indian policymakers.

Epilogue

This brings us to the end of this short, introductory volume to public policy in India. After a hurricane survey of the field of public policy and its evolution in India, we attempted to point out a few key concerns to flag its wide coverage. Next, we looked at the three broad steps of policymaking—formulation, implementation, and analysis—in some details, devoting a chapter to each. In the final chapter, we focused on some of the key shifts and national challenges that should claim the attention of the policymaker in India in these changing times.

Needless to say, this has been, at best a 10,000 feet view of the policymaking context in India. We have made no attempt at comprehensiveness. Several competing questions and topics have had to be reluctantly set aside to maintain the brevity of the volume. The purpose of the book has been to set the curious reader on a journey to understand a subject whose result already affects a large part of his or her life. The aim was not to be the last word of a vast and continuously evolving subject.

If we have succeeded in piquing the interest of the readers in continuing on this journey of discovery, it would not be out of place here to suggest a few enjoyable, and yet very instructive volumes, as suggested further reading. Kaushik Basu's (2015) *An Economist in the Real World*, from the MIT Press, would help understand the nuances of policymaking with his characteristic wit. Arun Maira's (2014) *Redesigning the Aeroplane While Flying: Reforming Institutions*, from Rupa is another excellent source of understanding broad issues. Those interested in studying implementation may benefit from Rajesh Chakrabarti's (2012), *Bihar Breakthrough: The Turnaround of a Beleagured State* from Rupa, parts of which we have drawn upon here as examples. Devesh Kapur and Pratap Bhanu Mehta's (2007) *Public Institutions in India: Performance and Design* from Oxford University Press India provides key insights on the institutional factors that help in the growth of the economy. Bibek Debroy, Ashley Tellis, and Reece Trevor (2014) edited *Getting India Back on Track: An Action Agenda for Reform*, from Random House India, provides an excellent overview of contemporary policy challenges in India. Finally, at the risk of self-promotion, we would like to humbly also suggest keeping your eyes open for a volume from us tentatively titled *Shaping Policy in India: Alliance, Advocacy, and Activism* (Oxford University Press, forthcoming) that presents case studies of the emergence of nine major laws to understand how well the Indian context fits existing political theories. Happy reading!

Bibliography

Anand, S. 2007. 'Not Quite Like Us', *Tehelka*, 4(45).

Ayyar, R.V.V. 2009. *Pubic Policymaking in India*. New Delhi: Person Longman.

Banerjee, Abhijit Vinayak, and Esther Duflo. 2011. *Poor Economics: A Radical Rethinking of the Way to Fight Global Poverty*. New York: PublicAffairs.

Banerjee, Abhijit Vinayak, Esther Duflo, Rachel Glennerster, and Dhruva Kothari. 2010. 'Improving Immunisation Coverage in Rural India: Clustered Randomised Controlled Evaluation of Immunisation Campaigns with and without Incentives', *British Medical Journal*, 340: c2220.

Basu, Kaushik. 2015. *An Economist in the Real World: The Art of Policymaking in India*. Boston: MIT Press.

Cairney, Paul. 2011. *Understanding Public Policy, Theories and Issues*. London: Palgrave Macmillan.

Chakrabarti, Rajesh. 2012. *Bihar Breakthrough: The Turnaround of a Beleaguered State*. New Delhi: Rupa Publications.

Chakrabarti, R. and K. Sanyal. n.d. *Shaping Laws in India: Alliance, Advocacy, and Activism*. New Delhi: Oxford University Press (forthcoming).

Chaudhuri, Anindya. 2016. 'Bringing Knowledge Back In: Connecting Public Policy to Public Policy in India', *Economic and Political Weekly*, 51(23): 59–68.

Debroy, Bibek, Ashley Tellis, and Reece Trevor (eds). 2014. *Getting India Back on Track: An Action Agenda for Reform*. New Delhi: Random House India.

Drèze, Jean. 2002. 'On Research and Action', *Economic and Political Weekly*, 37(9): 817–19.

Dye, Thomas R. 1992. *Understanding Public Policy*, Seventh edition. Englewood Cliffs, NJ: Prentice Hall.

Economic Times. 2015. 'Vice-President Hamid Ansari upset over drafting error in Indo-Bangladesh land boundary Bill', 9 May. Available at http://articles.economictimes.indiatimes.com/2015-05-09/news/61977526_1_profit-bill-drafting-error-seemandhra, last accessed on 15 February 2016.

Greenstone, M., S. Harish, A. Sudarshan, and R. Pande. 2016. 'Yes Delhi, It worked', 19 January. Available at https://epic.uchicago.edu/news-events/news/yes-delhi-it-worked, last accessed on 15 February 2016.

Jain, Dipti. 2014. 'The Slow Moving Wheels of Indian Judiciary: An Overburdened Judicial System is Taking Longer to Dispose Cases', Livemint, 6 August. Available at http://www.livemint.com/Opinion/

VlqmTLJ1UzNtmKd7BuRVbM/The-slow-moving-wheels-of-Indian-judiciary.html, last accessed on 15 February 2016.

Kapur, Devesh. 2012. 'Capability Trap of the Indian State', presentation. Available at http://indiachinainstitute. org/wp-content/uploads/2012/10/Devesh-Kapur-PPT-4.28.2012.pdf, last accessed on 15 February 2016.

Kapur, Devesh and Pratap Bhanu Mehta. 2007. *Public Institutions in India: Performance and Design*. New Delhi: Oxford University Press.

Keynes, John Maynard. 1936. *The General Theory of Employment, Interest and Money*. London: Macmillan.

Khilnani, S. 2015. 'India's Rise: The Search for Wealth and Power in the 21st Century', in David M. Malone, C. Raja Mohan, and Srinath Raghavan (eds), *The Oxford Handbook of Indian Foreign Policy*, pp. 681–98. Oxford: Oxford University Press.

Maira, Arun. 2014. *Redesigning the Aeroplane While Flying: Reforming Institutions*. New Delhi: Rupa Publications.

Mathur, Kuldeep. 2013. *Public Policy and Politics in India: How Institutions Matter*. New Delhi: Oxford University Press.

Mathur, Aneesha. 2016. 'JNU row: Kanhaiya Kumar gets bail and a lesson on thoughts that "infect… (like) gangrene"', *Indian Express*, 3 March. Available at http://indianexpress. com/article/india/india-newsindia/kanhaiya-kumar-bail-jnu-delhi-high-court/, last accessed in March 2016.

Ministry of Finance. 2016. *Economic Survey 2016–17*. New Delhi: Government of India.

Ministry of Law and Justice. 2014. 'Decision Taken in the meeting of the Committee of Secretaries held on 10th January, 2014 under the Chairmanship of Cabinet Secretary on Pre-legislative Consultation Policy', Letter by the Law Department, 5 February. Available at http://lawmin.nic.in/ld/plcp.pdf, last accessed on 15 February 2016.

Mohan, Archis. 2013. 'Indian Diplomacy Fails Numbers Test', StratPost, 1 October. Available at http://www.stratpost.com/indian-diplomacy-fails-numbers-test, last accessed on 15 February 2016.

Kingdon, John W. 1995. *Agendas, Alternatives and Public Policies*, Second edition. Addison–Wesley Educational Publishers Inc., USA.

Muralidharan, Karthik, Paul Niehaus, and Sandip Sukhtankar. n.d. 'Building State Capacity: Evidence from Biometric Smartcards in India', *American Economic Review*, forthcoming.

Muralidharan, Karthik and Nishith Prakash. 2013. 'Cycling to School: Increasing Secondary School Enrollment for Girls in India', *NBER Working Paper*, No. 19305. Available at http://www.nber.org/papers/w19305, last accessed on 15 February 2016.

Prasad, Chandra Bhan, D. Shyam Babu, Devesh Kapur, and Lant Pritchett. 2010. 'Rethinking Inequality: Dalits in

Uttar Pradesh in the Market Reform Era', *Economic and Political Weekly*, 45(35): 39–49.

Narayan, O.P. (ed.). 2005. *Harnessing Child Development: Children and the Right to Education.* New Delhi: Isha Books.

Rajasekhar, D., Erlend Berg, Maitreesh Ghatak, R. Manjula, and Sanchari Roy. 2011. 'Implementing Health Insurance: The Rollout of Rashtriya Swasthya Bima Yojana in Karnataka', *Economic and Political Weekly*, 46(20): 56–63.

Raju, K.V. and A. Ravindra. 2016. 'Promoting Policy Formulation at the State Level in India', FPI's Journal of Economics and Governance, Aarthika Charche, *FPI's Journal of Economics and Governance*, 1(1): 11–18.

Ramesh, J. 2015. *Green Signals: Ecology, Growth, and Democracy in India.* New Delhi: Oxford University Press.

Second Administrative Reforms Commission. 2008. *Refurbishing of Personnel Administration: Scaling New Heights*, Government of India. Available at http://arc.gov.in/10th/ARC_10th_report.htm, last accessed on 15 February 2016.

Shankar, Apoorva. 2014. 'Parliament's Role in Financial Oversight', Discussion Paper, PRS Legislative Research. Available at http://www.prsindia.org/parliamenttrack/discussion-papers/parliaments-role-in-financial-oversight-3478/, last accessed on 15 February 2016.

Stoker, G. 1998. 'Governance as Theory: Five Propositions', *International Social Science Journal*, 50: 17–28.

Stone, Deborah. 2012. *Policy Paradox: The Art of Political Decision Making*, Third edition. New York: W.W. Norton & Company.

Tang, Amy, Evan Rankin, Brendan de Caires, and Drew Beesley. 2015. 'Imposing Silence: The Use of India's Laws to Suppress Free Speech', PEN International. Available at http://www.pen-international.org/wp-content/uploads/2015/05/Imposing-Silence-4-WEB.pdf, last accessed on 15 February 2016.

Weiner, Myron. 1979a. 'Social Science Research and Public Policy in India', *Economic and Political Weekly*, 14(37): 1579–87.

———. 1979b. 'Social Science Research and Public Policy', *Economic and Political Weekly*, 14(38): 1622–8.

Wike, Richard and Katie Simmons. 2015. 'Global Support for Principle of Free Expression, but Opposition to Some Forms of Speech: Americans Especially Likely to Embrace Individual Liberties', Pew Research Center, 18 November. Available at http://www.pewglobal.org/2015/11/18/global-support-for-principle-of-free-expression-but-opposition-to-some-forms-of-speech/, last accessed in March 2016.

Yadav, Yogendra. 2008. 'The Paradox of Political Representation', *Seminar*, 586. Available at http://www.india-seminar.com/2008/586/586_yogendra_yadav.htm, last accessed on 15 February 2016.

Index

2G scam, 54, 161; 2G
    spectrum, 21
3ie (multinational
    consulting outfit), 115

Aadhaar cards, 126–7, 154,
    157
Aam Aadmi Party (AAP),
    21, 157
Abdul Latif Jameel Poverty
    Action Lab (J-PAL), 115
Abhayanand, xi–xiv
abhiyan (mission), 96
academia–government
    connect, 144
ActionAid, 15
administrative machinery,
    structure of, 76–8;
    district-level, 79–80

Administrative Reforms
    Commissions (ARCs),
    153, 156, 158
advocacy coalition
    framework (ACF), 37
agenda-setting, process of,
    50–6
AIDS, 133
alimony, right to, 28
American Evaluation
    Association (AEA), 115
Andhra Pradesh, 20, 51,
    101, 126
animal habitats, protection
    of, 60
*Annual Status of Education
    Report (ASER),* 123,
    125
Ansari, Hamid, 148

anti–child–labour
movement, 146
Anti–Defection law (1984),
66
Asian Development
Research Institute
(ADRI), 135
Aspiring Minds, 163
ASSOCHAM, 136
Australia, 148, 151–2, 160,
163
Ayodhya, 28
Azamgarh, 140

Babri Masjid, 28
*bahubali*s, xiii
Banerjee, Abhijeet, 120–1
Banerjee, Mamata, 66
Bankruptcy Law Reforms
Committee, 59
Basu, Kaushik, 130, 132
below poverty line (BPL)
cards, 20
Bhabha, Homi, 10
Bharti Institute of Public
Policy, 15
Bhartiya Janata Party (BJP),
28

bicycle programme, 129
Bihar, 81, 100–8
Bihar Vikas Mission, 157
Bill and Melinda Gates
Foundation, 115, 133
bill drafting, process of, 58
Billion Prices Project, 160
bounded rationality,
concept of, 37
Brookings Institution, 8, 15
Brookings, Robert S., 8
Bt brinjal, commercial
testing of, 146–7
Bulandshahar, 140
bureaucracy, 60–1, 75, 92–4,
102–4, 131
Bureau of Economic
Analysis, 160
Bureau of Justice Statistics,
160
Bureau of Labor Statistics,
160
Bureau of the Census, 160
business process outsourcing
(BPO), 163

Cabinet Secretariat, 58, 99,
157

Cameron, James, 23
Campaign Against Child
    Labour (1992), 51
Canada, 29, 115, 148, 177
capacity building, in
    administration, 156–8
capital investment, 165
Carleton, Canada, 115
Carleton University, 115
Carnegie Endowment, 8,
    15
Carnegie India, 15
caste-based discrimination,
    24–5
caste identity, 146
Central Bureau of
    Investigation (CBI), 85,
    92
Central Statistical
    Organization (CSO),
    159
Central Vigilance
    Commission (CVC),
    85, 92
Centre for Civil Society
    (CCS), 16, 134
Centre for Competition,
    Investment and

Economic Regulation of
    the Consumer Unity and
    Trust Society (CUTS-
    CCIER), 134
Centre for Legislative
    Research and Advocacy,
    157
Centre for Policy Research
    (CPR), 16
Chanakya's *Arthashastra*, 4
Chandigarh, 139
change, theory of, 130
Chelliah, Raja, 11
child labour, 35, 51, 166–7
Child Rights and You
    (CRY), 52
China, 16, 87, 162–3, 165
CII, 136
citizenship rights, 145
civil services examination,
    87
civil society activism, 57
civil society agitations, 30
civil society organizations,
    53, 95, 146
Climate Policy Initiative
    (CPI), 133–5
coal-block scam, 54, 92

collective welfare, principle of, 19

Common Minimum Programme, 62

common service centres (CSCs), 155

communication skills, 8

Companies Act (2013), 61

Companies Law Committee, 61

Competition Act (2002), 148

Comptroller and Auditor General (CAG), 85, 92

Congressional Budget Office, 8, 152

Congressional Research Service (CRS), 151

Constitution of India, 48–9; amendments of 1992, 73rd and 74th, 49; Constitution (86th Amendment) Act (2002), 57; Constitution (93rd Amendment) Bill (2001), 57; schedule 12 of, 49–50

corporate bankruptcy, 59

corruption, 91, 104, 132, 155

Criminal Law (Amendment) Act (2013), 63

crisis management, 153

CWG scam, 54

decision-making, 3, 5, 19, 30

Delhi Dialogue Commission, 157

Delhi Metro, 97

Delhi Rent Act (1995), 69

Demands for Grants, 150

democratic deficit, 162

Departmentally Related Standing Committee (DRSCs), 64–5, 68; on Demands for Grants, 150

Department for International Development (DFID), UK, 115, 126, 134–5

Department of Personnel and Training (DoPT), 12

Devanagare, 75

difference-in-difference
method, 122
Directive Principles of State
Policy, 39, 49
disaster management, 97;
standard operating
procedure (SOP) of, 97
distributive justice, principle
of, 20–5
Dongria Kondh tribe, 23
drafting of public policy,
process of, 57–62
Drèze, Jean, 93
Duflo, Esther, 120–1

'Ease of Doing Business'
index, 164
East India Company, 88
economic development, 5;
benefits of, 23
economic liberalization of
India, 160
economy, information-
driven, 158
e-governance, 32–3, 85, 91,
154–5
Eighth Five Year Plan, 142
Eklavya, 52

elected legislature, authority
of, 31
emerging market
economies, 5
empowerment, with
monitoring, 101
The Energy and Resources
Institute (TERI)
University, 13
Energy Policy Institute
of Chicago (EPIC),
University of Chicago,
114
Engineering Services
Examination, 87
Eritrea, 139
e-services, 155
ethics and fiscal
management, 153
evidence-based
policymaking, benefit
of, 130
Evidence for Policy Design
(EPoD), Harvard, 114

federalism, features of,
40–1
Federal Reserve, 166

Federation of Indian
    Chambers of Commerce
    and Industry (FICCI),
    61, 136
FedStats, 160
Financial Sector Legislative
    Reforms Commission,
    55
Finland, 160
Food Safety and Standards
    Act (2006), 69
food security: issue of, 22,
    60; laws and legislation
    governing, 62
forced labour, in factories, 35
foreign direct investment
    (FDI), 14
formulation–
    implementation–analysis
    cycle, 137
free speech, fundamental
    right to, 26–7, 29
Friedman, Tom, 165
fundamental rights, directive
    principles of, 39, 48–9

G-20, 140
Gandhi, Mahatma, 19

Gandhi, Rajiv, 28, 92
Gazette of India, 69
GDP, 140–1, 164
Germany, 29, 140
global financial system, 167
*Global Go-To Think Tank
    Index Report,* 16
globalization: country's
    economy, impact on,
    166; and its political
    fallout, 165–7
good governance, concept
    of, 142
Government of India, 12
Government Performance
    Management, 155–6
government policies,
    independent evaluation
    of, 17
Gujarat, 101
Gurgaon, 122

Harvard Business School, 6
Harvard's Kennedy School
    of Government, 8, 12
Hazare, Anna, 54–5
High Court, 21, 26, 32, 48,
    148

Hindu Centre for Politics and Public Policy, 15–16
Hindu Group, 15
Hindu personal laws, 28
hospital empanelment, 82
House of Representatives, 151

Ideas for India, 136
Independent Evaluation Office (IEO), 114, 116
'India Against Corruption' movement, 54, 63
India Development Foundation (IDF), 16
Indian Administrative Services (IAS), 86, 88
Indian Council for Research on International Economic Relations (ICRIER), 16
Indian Economic Service, 87
Indian Institute of Dalit Studies, 24
Indian Institute of Science (IISC), 13

Indian Institutes of Management (IIMs), 11–12; Centre for Public Policy (CPP), 12; IIM Ahmedabad (IIMA), 13; IIM Bangalore (IIMB), 12; IIM Kolkata, 12; JSW School of Public Policy, 15; postgraduate programme on public policy and management (PGPPPM), 12; public management and policy (PGP-PMP), 13
Indian Police Service (IPS), xi, 88
Indian School of Business (ISB), 15
Indian Statistical Institute, 135
Indian Statistical Service, 87
India's policymakers, challenges for: averting demographic disaster, 162–5; demographic dividend, harnessing of, 162–5; globalization and

its political fallout, 165–7; regulating of private sector, 160–2

India's political structure, features of: federalism, 40–1; fundamental rights and directive principles, 48–9; local self-governance, 49–50; separation of powers, 41–8

individual property rights, 23

individual's rights: balancing of, 25–9; principle of, 19

industry–government relationship, 14

information technology (IT), 85, 100; use of, 154

Information Technology Act, 25

Infosys, 157

Insolvency and Bankruptcy Code (2015), 59–60

Institute of Chartered Accountants of India (ICAI), 61

Institute of Cost Accountants of India (ICMAI), 61

Institute of Defence Studies and Analyses (IDSA), 16

insurance agencies, selection of, 82

International Growth Centre (IGC), 132, 134–6

international trade, 4

Internet, 85, 167

Ireland, 160

Islamic State of Iraq and Syria (ISIS), 164

Jain, Mohini, 51

Jan Lokpal campaign, 54, 56

*jan-sunwai*s (public hearings), 53, 94–5

*janta darbar*s, 105

Jat agitation (2016), 21, 25, 165

Jawaharlal Nehru University (JNU), New Delhi, 167

Jharkhand, 129, 153

John F. Kennedy School of Government, 8
Jones, B.D., 37
J-PAL, 120–1
JSW School of Public Policy, 15
Judges (Disclosure of Assets and Liabilities) Bill, 64
judicial activism, 32–3

Karnataka, 33, 51, 75, 79, 153–4
Kashmir, 164
Kautilya, 91
Kejriwal, Arvind, 54
Keynes, John Maynard, 130
khap panchayats, 35
Kingdon, John, 53
Kullu, 75, 80
Kumar, Kanhaiya, 25–6
Kumar, Nitish, xi, 101–8, 128
Kumbh Mela, 96

labour management, 153
Laine, James, 25
land acquisition law (2013), 149

land revenue, collection of, 90
Lasswell, Harold, 3; model for policy formulation, 37; public policy, definition of, 19
Law Commission, 55
Lee Kuan Yew School of Public Policy, Singapore, 8
legislative capability, 150–2
Lerner, Daniel, 3
Liberty Institute, 8
Library of Congress, 160
Lindblom, Charles, 37
Lokayuktas, 156
Lokpal and Lokayuktas Act (2013), 63, 64
Lok Sabha, 60, 64, 68, 162
London School of Economics, 132

Machiavelli's *Prince,* 4
Madhya Pradesh, 153
Mahalnobis, P.C., 10
Mahatma Gandhi National Rural Employment

Guarantee Scheme
(MGNREGS), 119,
126; method of fund
distribution in, 127
Management Development
Institute (MDI), India,
13
management, development
of, 1
management information
system (MIS), 98
management programme in
public policy (MPPP),
15
Maoist insurgency, 164
Massachusetts Institute of
Technology (MIT), 115,
120; Abdul Latif Jameel
Poverty Action Lab
(J-PAL), 115; Billion
Prices Project, 160
Master of Business
Administration (MBA),
163
Mazdoor Kisan Shakti
Sangathan, 94
media, role in shaping
public policy, 56

Meerut, 51
members of Parliament
(MPs), 48, 68, 150
microfinance industry,
regulation of, 60
microfinance institutions
(MFI), 60
Ministry of Finance, 59
Ministry of Health and
Family Welfare, 81
Ministry of Labour and
Employment, 81
Ministry of Law and Justice,
59
Ministry of Statistics
and Programme
Implementation, 159;
National Sample Survey
Office (NSSO), 159
minority rights, protection
of, 27
mixed methods, 123
MNREGA, 62
Modi, Narendra, 61–2, 101
Moily, Veerappa, 153
monetary policy of India,
167
money bills, 64

multiple streams approach, 38

Muralidharan, Karthik, 126

MV Foundation, 52

Naidu, Chandrababu, 101

National Advisory Council (NAC), 62, 147

National Alliance for the Fundamental Right to Education (NAFRE), 52

National Association of Software and Service Companies (NASSCOM), 163

National Council of Applied Economic Research (NCAER), 16

National Democratic Alliance (NDA), 81

National Employability Report for Engineering Graduates (2015), 163

National Food Security Act (NFSA), 31

National Health Insurance Scheme, 72

National Human Rights Commission, 55

National Informatics Centre (NIC), 158

National Investigation Agency Bill (2008), 64

National Sample Survey Office (NSSO), 159

National University of Singapore, 8

natural resources, allocation of, 161

Nehru, Jawaharlal, 10–11, 28

New Delhi Municipal Council (NDMC), 98

New Zealand, 151

Nilekani, Nandan, 156–7

'Nirbhaya' rape case, 54, 56

NITI Aayog, 62, 116

Niyamgiri dispute, 22–4

non-governmental organizations (NGOs), 15, 23, 40, 52

non-profit special interest groups, 132

non-state actors, role of, 63–4

North-East, 164
Norway, 160
'not in employment,
    education, or training'
    (NEET) population, 164

'ObamaCare' healthcare
    plan, 5
Observer Research
    Foundation (ORF), 16
'odd–even' rule, of vehicular
    rationing, 109, 112;
    effect on pollution,
    112–14
Odisha, 22
Odisha Mining
    Corporation, 22
Office for Budget
    Responsibility, 152
Office of the Parliamentary
    Council of the UK,
    149–50
O.P. Jindal Global
    University, Sonipat,
    Haryana, 15
ordinances, power of, 148
Organisation for Economic
    Co-operation and

Development (OECD),
    159–60
other backward classes
    (OBC), 21
Oxfam, 15

Panchayati Raj system, 49,
    90, 94
Parakh, P.C., 92
Parivartan (non-
    governmental
    organization), 94
parliamentary form, of
    government, 38
Parliamentary Research
    Service, 31
participative policymaking:
    for better formulation
    of policy, 148–52; for
    better policy analysis,
    158–60; for creating the
    right environment for
    collaboration, 144–7;
    towards more effective
    implementation, 152–8
passage of Bills, in
    Parliament, 64–6
Patel, I.G., 11

Patna, xi
Pew Research Center,
    Washington, DC, 29
Plain Writing Act (2010),
    149
Planning Commission,
    61–2, 116, 125
policy adoption, process of,
    62–70
policy advocacy, 131–7;
    advocacy groups, 132–3
policy analysis and
    evaluation: challenges
    in, 109–16; convincing
    with, 131–7; 'difference-
    in-difference' method,
    122; different methods
    of, 116–25; role of,
    109–16; studies about
    India, 125–31
policy changes, human
    effects of, 125
policy entrepreneurs, 53
policy formulation, process
    of, 36–7; articulation
    stage (drafting), 57–62;
    identification stage
    (agenda-setting), 50–6;

policy adoption stage,
    62–70
policy implementation:
    administrative
    turnarounds for, 100–8;
    bureaucratic practice
    of, 99; capability
    constraint, impact of,
    85–95; case study of
    Bihar (2005–12), 100–8;
    challenges for, 81–5, 100;
    incentive/motivation
    for, 90–5; management
    of, 95–100; mechanism
    of, 74; neglect of, 92–3;
    quality of, 91, 100; results
    framework document
    (RFD) approach for, 99;
    strategy for, 81
policy interventions, studies
    of, 131
policymaking: civil society
    participation in, 147;
    coordination and access
    to information for,
    158–60; evidence-based,
    130; in India, 10; need to
    broad-base participation

in, 146–7; participative
See participative
policymaking; process of,
39; stages of, 6, 38
policy-oriented learning, 38
'policy sciences' paradigm, 7
Policy Sciences, The (1951), 3
polio eradication campaign,
96
political science, 2
pollution control, 32,
111–13
Poor Economics (2011), 120
'pork-barrel' politics,
practice of, 30
poverty alleviation, 111
practical relevance, 2
Pratham, 52, 125
Preamble of the
Constitution, 19, 22,
25; Forty-second
Constitutional
Amendment, 27
presidential system, of
political structure, 48
PRS Legislative Research,
157
public administration, 2–4

public contract, 144–6
Public Distribution System
(PDS), 21, 60
public interest litigations
(PIL), 31, 53, 56, 94
public management, 12
public policy: definitions
of, 4, 19; education and
research in, 12–15; field
of, 1–10; formulation
and analysis of, 3, 40;
as guide to decision-
making, 3; idea and
practice of, 142;
implementation of, 6;
in India, 10–18; making
of, 6; media, role of, 56;
schools of, 3; subject
matter of, 3; training, 13
public policy debates,
in India, 18–34; on
distributive justice, 20–5;
on individual's rights,
25–9; on settlement of
policy, 30–4
public policy programmes,
subjects and
specializations in, 9

Public Private Partnership (PPP), 154–5
Public Service Commission (PSC), 13
public service delivery, 85, 100, 144; accountability for, 155–6; improvement of, 152–6; PPP model of, 154–5
public services, right to, 153–4
punctuated equilibrium framework, theory of, 38

quality of laws, improvement of, 148–50

Rajasthan, 32, 93, 121, 134
Rajasthan Sun Technique Concentrated Solar Power (CSP) Plant, in Rajasthan, 134
Rajya Sabha, 60, 64, 68, 149
Ramesh, Jairam, 146
Ram Janmabhoomi–Babri Masjid dispute, 28

RAND Corporation, 8
randomized control trials (RCT), 117, 119, 129
Rao, V.K.R.V., 10
rape laws, 54
Rashtriya Swasthya Bima Yojana (RSBY), 72, 81, 82–4; financing of, 84
religious freedom, right to, 27
religious minorities, rights of, 28
religious nationalism, 146
renewable energy, adoption of, 134
renewable policy initiatives, 134
renewable sources of energy, 134
Reserve Bank of India (RBI), 70
resource allocation, problem of, 22
Results-Framework-Document (RFD) method of Performance Evaluation, 157

Right to Education (RTE), 5, 49, 51–2; RTE Act, 31, 57, 147

Right to Food Security, 21, 49, 146

Right to Information (RTI), 85, 92, 146; RTI Act, 33

rural development, 89

Rushdie, Salman, 25; *Satanic Verses, The,* 25

Sabatier, Paul, 37

'Sahaj e-Village' initiative, 155

'Sakala' initiative, Karnataka, 33

SAKALA Services Act, 154

San Francisco, 133

Satyarthi, Kailash, 167

Sciences Po, Paris, France, 8

secularism, definition of, 27

select laws and Bills, timelines of, 67

self-governance, local, 49–50; devolution of powers, 50

Senate, 70, 151

Sengupta, Arjun, 11

separation of powers, doctrine of, 32, 41–8, 148

sexual harassment, prevention of, 31–2

Shah Bano case, 28

skill development, challenge of, 164

skilled policy activists, 53

social media, 112

Social Security Pension (SSP), 126

Soros, George, 133

South Africa, 160

South Korea, 163

Soviet Union, 10

Special Economic Zones Bill (2005), 64

Sreedharan, E., 97

SREI Infrastructure Ltd, 155; 'Sahaj e-Village' initiative, 155

Srikrishna, B.N., 55

state administration, improvement of, 100

State Public Service Commissions, 13

St.Vincent and the
    Grenadines, 139
Sun, Tzu, 4; *Art of War,*
    The, 4
Supreme Court, 21, 25, 28,
    32, 48, 51–2, 109, 127,
    148, 161
Swachh Bharat Abhiyan,
    62
Swaniti, 157
Sweden, 160

Tata Institute of
    Fundamental Research
    (TIFR), 13
Tata Institute of Social
    Sciences (TISS), 13
tax employees, 87
Tehelka, 24
Tenth Five Year Plan
    (2002–7), 143
Thackeray, Bal, 25
third party administrator
    (TPA), 84
tribal population: customary
    rights of, 23; economic
    development, benefits of,
    23; resource allocation

to, 23; rights to forest
    land, 60; socio–cultural
    ethos of, 24
Trinamool Congress party,
    66
Trivedi, Prajapati, 157

UK Evaluators' Society
    (UKES), 115
UN Evaluations Group
    (UNEG), 114
uniform civil code, 49
Union Public Service
    Commission (UPSC),
    13
Unique Identification
    Authority of India
    (UIDAI), 157
Unique Reference Number
    (URN), 83
United Nations
    Development
    Programme (UNDP), 12
United Nations Office
    on Drugs and Crime
    (UNODC), 86
United Progressive Alliance
    (UPA), 21, 31, 62, 147

United States Agency
for International
Development (USAID),
115
University of California,
San Diego, 126
University of Chicago, 114
University of Minnesota,
167
University of Pennsylvania,
16
Unnikrishnan case (1993),
51–2
USA, 16, 152, 163
Uttar Pradesh, 140

Vishaka judgment, 32
Vishwanathan, T.K., 59
Voice of India, 52

welfare state, emergence
of, 5
Westminster (British)
model, of political
structure, 48
Wilson, Woodrow, 2
World Bank, 114, 125–6,
130, 142, 157

Yadav, Yogendra, 145
yatras, 105

About the Authors

.

RAJESH CHAKRABARTI is a co-founder and director at the Gurgaon-based policy research start-up, Sunay Policy Advisory Pvt. Ltd (www.sunayadvisory.com). Previously, Chakrabarti taught at the University of Alberta, Canada; Georgia Tech, Atlanta, USA; and the Indian School of Business (ISB), Hyderabad, India. He was the Executive Vice President, Research and Policy at the Wadhwani Foundation, besides holding visiting positions at the Indian Statistical Institute, Indian Institute of Management Calcutta, and the Federal Reserve Bank, Atlanta, among others. As the founding executive director of the Bharti Institute of Public Policy at ISB's Mohali campus, he set up one of the country's few policy research institutions and designed and launched the Management Programme in Public

Policy (MPPP). He has written as well as edited six and published several scholarly articles. Chakrabarti is an alumnus of Presidency College, Calcutta, Indian Institute of Management, Ahmedabad, and has a PhD from the University of California, Los Angeles, USA.

KAUSHIKI SANYAL is a co-founder and CEO of Sunay Policy Advisory Pvt. Ltd. Her former and current clients include the World Bank, Vidhi Centre for Legal Policy, Rajiv Gandhi Foundation, and the Kamonohashi Project, Japan. She has been a senior analyst at the Bharti Institute of Public Policy at ISB where she supervised a variety of research projects commissioned by multilateral agencies such as UNDP, UNICEF, and the World Bank. She played a key role in developing the MPPP and lectured in it as a visiting faculty. She has been one of earliest team members at PRS Legislative Research. Sanyal has published multiple articles in journals including *Economic and Political Weekly* as well as book chapters and writes regularly in leading newspapers. A political science alumnus of Lady Shri Ram College, she has an MA and PhD from the Jawaharlal Nehru University.

The husband–wife co-authors live in New Delhi and love to travel. Their forthcoming volume, *Shaping Laws in India: Alliance, Advocacy, and Activism*, analyses, using case studies of the evolution of nine landmark laws, the lawmaking process in India.